Liberal Education and Democratic Citizenship

Liberal Education and Democratic Citizenship

Michael H. McCarthy

LEXINGTON BOOKS
Lanham • *Boulder* • *New York* • *London*

Published by Lexington Books
An imprint of The Rowman & Littlefield Publishing Group, Inc.
4501 Forbes Boulevard, Suite 200, Lanham, Maryland 20706
www.rowman.com

86-90 Paul Street, London EC2A 4NE

British Library Cataloguing in Publication Information Available

Library of Congress Cataloging-in-Publication Data

ISBN 978-1-66694-877-6 (cloth: alk. paper)
ISBN 978-1-66694-878-3 (ebook)

∞™ The paper used in this publication meets the minimum requirements of American National Standard for Information Sciences—Permanence of Paper for Printed Library Materials, ANSI/NISO Z39.48-1992.

Contents

Preface

This book has emerged from the intersection of two powerful and enduring commitments: my long life as a student and teacher of the liberal arts, and my active engagement as a citizen of the United States. I began my liberal education at Notre Dame in 1959, where I focused my studies on the reading and discussion of the great books. Deeply inspired by my teachers and the example of my friends, I pursued a doctorate in philosophy at Yale University when my college years ended. Yale also had wonderful courses and a distinguished faculty who encouraged me to become a teacher/scholar when I completed my doctoral studies.

Between studying at Notre Dame and Yale, I explored the countries and cultures of Western Europe, received six months of Infantry training in the American South, and began a six-year period of service with the Connecticut and New York National Guard. Thus, my life as an engaged and reflective citizen and my commitment to a career of learning and teaching began at the same time, and continue uninterrupted to the present day.

I cast my first vote for Lyndon Johnson in the presidential election of 1964, watched his Great Society initiatives falter in the jungles of Vietnam, and fully embraced Johnson's defining commitment to equal and enforceable rights for all of our citizens. I also watched Roosevelt's New Deal coalition collapse during our first years at Vassar, as both Southern and Northern Democrats rejected the high demands of a fully multiracial and just society. That collapse eventually led to the Republican party's "Southern Strategy" and the shift of white working-class loyalties from the party of Roosevelt to the party of Reagan. With that shift has come an intense and unresolved argument about the importance and limits of government, and the rights and responsibilities of democratic citizens.

But the political debate about personal and public liberty has coincided with an equally important cultural argument about the nature and purpose of liberal education. What is a *liberal* education; what essential goods does it seek to promote and preserve; how closely is it connected to the formation of

responsible democratic citizens; and what are the personal and public consequences of neglecting its centrality and enduring importance?

After nearly sixty years as a teacher and citizen, I've come to believe that
at the core of both of these arguments is the complex question of human
freedom. A question that can only be answered comprehensively by a mature
account of the human person, human nature, the human condition, and the
essential stages of human becoming and flourishing.

The personal account offered in this book, then, is the fruit of lifelong
reflection and action. I offer it now because our crises in democracy, education, and citizenship are deeply connected. And they demand, I believe, the
very best from us all, who know, love, and accept responsibility for the broken world we commonly share.

Michael McCarthy
Professor Emeritus of Philosophy
Vassar College

Introduction

AMERICAN DEMOCRACY AND CIVIC EDUCATION: WHERE ARE WE NOW?

Before the great eighteenth century revolutions in America and France, the defenders of self-government believed that it was a viable political strategy only for the few: the educated and economically independent citizens of a unified nation. But the American and French revolutions were historically transformative because they were waged on behalf of a radically new political ideal. In colonial America, the ideal of promoting and preserving equal liberty and justice for all citizens. In monarchical France, the ideal of securing liberty, equality, and fraternity among all the members of the new French republic.

Now, we know historically that these inspirational ideals have never been actually achieved. In the United States, from the beginning, they were explicitly contradicted by chattel slavery, the abusive treatment of America's native peoples, economic and political injustice across competing social classes, and the evident failure to educate all our citizens, especially women, African Americans, religious minorities, and non-European immigrants for the full rights and responsibilities of democratic citizenship.[1]

The American struggle to create a just multiracial democracy has been complex and difficult. In the nearly two hundred and fifty years since our Declaration of Independence, we have waged and won a difficult war for independence from Great Britain. Created a Federal Constitution based on the separation and balance of political powers, executive, legislative, and judicial. And extended our national boundaries, not without violence, from the Atlantic to the Pacific, and from the Canadian border to the independent state of Mexico.

We also endured four years of bloody Civil War between the federal government and the secessionist states of the Confederacy. Yet, after victory in that war, we Americans permitted the defeated Southern states to create a system of Jim Crow, based on *de jure* racial inequality and systemic segregation. And we clearly accepted a pattern of *de facto* segregation in housing, employment, education, and social relationships throughout most of the rest of our country.[2]

We also suffered from the enduring tensions between our commitment to democracy and our attachment to capitalism. The Great Depression of the 1930s revealed the severe limits of unregulated capitalism and of the philosophical and political defense of minimal governmental engagement in the economy (*laissez-faire*). To achieve greater economic and social justice, Americans largely accepted a strong federal government under Franklin Roosevelt and Lyndon Johnson, who, together, gradually created a limited welfare state for our citizens. That democratic state included Social Security, Medicare, Medicaid, unemployment insurance, progressive taxation, and a shared commitment to health, education, and economic security for all Americans. It also included, under President Johnson, a strong federal commitment to civil rights and political liberty for African American citizens throughout the country[3]

Another critical American challenge concerned our country's relation to the rest of the world. Because of our geographic location across two oceans, Americans were originally isolationist in their foreign policy, particularly with respect to Europe and Asia. But in the twentieth century, we fought two victorious world wars that engaged our military forces across North Africa, Europe, and the South Pacific. And after the second war, we helped to create the United Nations and committed our country to multilateral defense alliances in both Europe and Asia. The creation of a unified national military able to wage war with our allies had uneven results. Sometimes successful (the two great world wars), sometimes not (Vietnam, the Middle East, Afghanistan). And now, with the end of the Cold War, the rise of Islamic militarism, the emergence of a powerful and unified China, the common threat of climate change, and the uneven effects of globalization, we are still struggling as a country to reach a revised consensus on a just and realistic foreign policy for the twenty-first century.[4]

Another source of national division concerns our attitudes to immigration and pluralism. The earliest European immigrants to North America were middle-class Protestants from Great Britain and the Netherlands. Later, they were followed by rural and urban Catholics from Ireland, Italy, and Central Europe. Then persecuted Jews from Eastern Europe and Imperial Russia. And eventually working-class immigrants from Asia, Latin America, and Africa. Often, the descendants of the original Americans were unwelcoming to the newcomers, who brought with them different languages, unfamiliar religious and cultural traditions, perceived economic competition, and the nativist suspicion that they were not loyal Americans. These different sources of pluralism, linguistic, cultural, religious and economic, fostered strong "nationalist" hostility, divisive demagoguery, outright violence (the Ku Klux Klan), and strict immigration quotas to exclude the "undesirables." They also increased the importance of the common civic education needed to unite Americans from such different cultural backgrounds. Not only the education received in schools, but also in a supportive civil society where the reality of *E pluribus unum* might be gradually achieved.[5]

During the last fifty years, all these sources of national division have converged and intensified. The continuing struggle for civil rights, the fierce divisions caused by the war in Vietnam, the protracted hostage taking in Iran, and the oil shocks and severe inflation of the late 1970s led to the collapse of the New Deal coalition and the rise of Ronald Reagan's economic and cultural conservatism. Reagan's was a backward-looking conservatism, based on low taxes, minimal governmental regulation of the economy, open sympathy with the formerly Democratic Southern states, and a direct appeal to evangelical Christians whose political loyalties had previously been equally divided between Democrats and Republicans. It was also a triumphalist conservatism that minimized America's moral and political failures in its celebration of American greatness.

Since Reagan's electoral triumph over President Carter, the competing priorities of our two great political parties have contributed to our political fragmentation. The national Democratic party has sought to preserve and extend the economic and social policies of the New Deal and the Great Society, to secure the civil rights of blacks, women, immigrants and ethnic minorities, and gradually to adapt to the increasing secularization of contemporary America. While the Republican party has sought to reduce or constrain the powers of the federal government in nearly every area but national defense, to support the regional sovereignty of state governments, and to reshape the federal judiciary in a narrow and highly partisan manner.

Other important factors poisoning the spirit of our politics in this post-Reagan era were the fiercely aggressive partisanship of Newt Gingrich, the fears created by the war on terror, the rise of white Christian nationalism, the ugly backlash against Barack Obama, the formation of the anti-immigrant Tea Party, the demagogic narcissism of Donald Trump and his Make America Great Again movement, and open and deliberate hostility to independent scientific inquiry in critical areas like global warming, vaccinations against infectious disease, and the crippling effects, social and cultural, of mounting economic inequality[6]

But in some ways, the greatest challenge to our national unity and the most formidable barrier to just and effective government are very closely related. Why? Because the educational, cultural, and institutional foundations of our democracy have been compromised. By a marked decline in civic education, excessive partisanship, deliberate lying and misinformation, the inordinate political and economic power of "dark money" and special interests, the direct assault on voting rights and fair elections, the partisan rejection of an impartial and trusted judiciary, the blatant attempt to divide our people by falsely discrediting those who disagree with "us." Portraying "them" as contemptuous of "our" inherited traditions and hostile to "our" rightful place in a free and just America.

Through these interrelated political and cultural failures, our democratic institutions and practices have lost their accepted legitimacy. And having lost it, they have also lost their effectiveness in addressing the grave challenges of our time.[7]

As a teacher, parent, and citizen, I have directly witnessed this mounting crisis in American democracy. As a college teacher, I have consistently tried to educate my students in the fundamentals of legitimate politics, the uneven history of democracies, especially American democracy, the many achievements and failures of our country, and the great importance and difficulty of achieving "liberty and justice for all." As parent and grandparent, I have tried to set a credible example as a husband, father, neighbor, and citizen. And as a responsible citizen, I have tried to serve my country, in both military and civilian life, by constantly learning about the world, honestly teaching about its greatness and wretchedness, and acting consistently for the common good.

With a troubled but hopeful spirit, I have also composed this book on *Liberal Education and Democratic Citizenship*. I hope to show the essential role that liberal education should play in creating informed and responsible citizens, and the dangerous consequences for our democracy when it fails to do so. And while I insist that civic education begins at home and is then sustained in the voluntary associations of civil society, I also believe it should culminate in a genuinely liberal education to be shared among all our citizens. For the existing crisis in our democracy concerns everyone: our political leaders, the political parties to which they belong, the public officials who serve in our government, both national and local media of communication, our educational, economic, and financial institutions, and the successive generations of citizens who together comprise the body politic. In other words, "we, the American people" as a whole. It is "we" who are in danger now[8]

This book is written then for both young and old. For students and teachers, parents and their maturing children, artists and scholars, journalists and the diverse audiences with whom they communicate, ordinary citizens and the political leaders they elect, assist, and hold accountable. While based on personal experience, it is also inspired by important political and educational commentary, ancient, modern and contemporary. The dialogues of Plato, the history of Thucydides, Aristotle's instructive essays on ethics and politics, Augustine's *Confessions,* Aquinas' Christian synthesis of both Aristotle and Augustine, Pascal's *Pensées*, De Tocqueville's *Democracy in America*, John Locke, Adam Smith, John Stuart Mill, and Immanuel Kant. Rousseau's

Second Discourse on the Origin of Inequality, Newman's *The Idea of a University*, Weber's *The Protestant Ethic and the Spirit of Capitalism* and *Politics as a Vocation*, Mark Van Doren's *Liberal Education*, Whitehead's *The Aims of Education* and *Science and the Modern World*, Werner Jaeger's *Paideia,* and Hannah Arendt's *The Origins of Totalitarianism, On Revolution,* and *Between Past and Future.* Bernard Lonergan's *Insight* and *Method in Theology*, Alasdair Macintyre's *After Virtue,* John Dunne's *The Way of All the Earth*, Robert Bellah's *Habits of the Heart*, Charles Taylor's *Sources of the Self* and *A Secular Age*, and Michael Sandel's *The Tyranny of Merit.* While I have drawn on the insights of many other writers and critics, these are the important thinkers to whom I am most indebted in this book.[9]

Before presenting my analysis of our democratic crisis, and the practical remedies I propose to address it, let me outline the unfolding of my argument and the critical distinctions on which it is based.

Chapter 1, "A House Divided Against Itself Cannot Stand," explores the sources, areas, and levels of division in contemporary America: racial, regional, gender based, cultural, economic, educational, religious, and generational. It also argues that these divisions create important disagreements about the major challenges facing us in today's globally interconnected world. And then reflects on how best to identify and address those challenges in a wise, generous, and effective manner.

As in the chapters that follow, I affirm both political constants grounded in human nature and the human condition, and political variables rooted in significant historical change. I also identify the different causes of political progress and decline, personal, cultural, and institutional. And confirm the fundamental importance of a sound civic education for all citizens, without which they cannot fulfill their responsibilities, personal and political, as mature adults. Chapter 1 is intended to establish a common framework and background for the important chapters that follow.

In chapter 2, "The Nature and Purpose of a Liberal Education," I draw on my long experience as a student and teacher of the liberal arts. And seek to articulate clearly what a liberal education is, and why it is so important, especially today, for both the students who receive it and the democratic communities they are educated to govern responsibly.[10]

A key distinction, relevant to many of the arguments in this book, is that between education and learning. Education is the deliberate process by which each community renews itself by creating a common fund of knowledge, a common set of arts and virtues, and a common store of truthful memories among its citizens. It is a temporally limited process that begins at birth and culminates with each citizen's developed readiness to meet the responsibilities of citizenship. A readiness cultivated by both the local and national community and oriented to achieving their present and future well-being (the common good).

Learning, by contrast, should continue for the whole of each person's life. It is grounded in and sustained by the individual's desire to know, to understand the world, both natural and historical, in its true complexity. When freely supported and encouraged, it leads to specialized knowledge and specialized communities of inquiry. In learning, the individual follows his/her personal passions and interests. In education, the community prepares all of its citizens for the obligations they will share as adults.[11]

A cooperative trinity makes liberal education possible. Dedicated teachers who know, love, and accept responsibility for the world, with all its greatness and wretchedness. Young students prepared to acquire a common set of arts and virtues under the supervision of their trusted teachers. And a common curriculum periodically revised by their teachers that reflects the changing state of knowledge and their changing appraisals of excellence and relevance in literature, the humanities and the arts. Once again, both constants grounded in human nature and the human condition, and significant changes grounded in our expanding knowledge of nature and human diversity, are at work. Creating an ever more inclusive community whose members learn to trust and respect each other as fellow citizens.[12]

But in what sense is this common education liberal? It is liberal because it is designed to cultivate effective freedom in a context of personal and cultural pluralism. Citizens become effectively free when they discover the causal interdependence of the world, learn how to recognize and enjoy the most important human goods, and commit themselves to promoting and preserving them together. In political terms, effective freedom is consistently devoted to the common good that requires liberty and justice for the whole community, and for both present and future generations of citizens ("thus fulfilling our fiduciary obligations to posterity").

The educated citizens in a democratic community are not blind to its faults and limitations. They recognize in themselves and their peers a constant susceptibility to bias. The individual bias that resists unwelcome truths and calmly accepts the violation of others' rights. That puts self-interest before the common good and justifies this moral inversion by invalid and unsound arguments. The group bias that privileges our race, class, gender, or religion against those of our fellow citizens, and then justifies this inequality by appealing to discursive prejudices without supporting evidence. And the general bias against the validity of specialized knowledge and its practical relevance to contested public policy debates, in areas like climate change, immigration, economic inequality, and preventive medicine.[13]

Liberal education deliberately promotes "critical belonging" to one's democratic community. It recognizes the importance of both rights and responsibilities, and acknowledges our common potential for both virtue and vice. It emphasizes the arts of language (the *trivium*) and the arts of measurement, and the many virtues essential to the good life, personal and public. Inclusive in spirit, alert to half-truths, false dichotomies and scapegoats, dedicated to justice and liberty, and critically aware of how hard they are to achieve, it is simultaneously realistic, persuasive, and hopeful.

Finally, to confirm its distinctive nature and importance, I appeal to the testimony of several great thinkers, ancient, modern and contemporary: Cicero, Bernard Lonergan, Cato, Hannah Arendt, Terence and Max Weber. They confirm the singular importance of the liberal arts (Cicero); our enduring need for disinterested knowledge (Lonergan); the complementarity of thought and action (Cato); our need for teachers who know and love both the world and the young (Arendt); the democratic respect for "other" persons and cultures (Terence and John Dunne); and the persistent dangers of a narrow individualism, technocratic or hedonistic (Max Weber).[14]

In chapter 3, "Demystifying the L-Word: the Merits and Limitations of Modern Liberalism," I seek to clarify the complex relationship between effective freedom and modern economic and political liberalism. To do this, I begin with the classical understanding of free persons and the medieval understanding of liberal studies. For the ancient Greeks and Romans, a free person was a male citizen capable of sharing in the high demands of self-government. In the medieval university, liberal studies focused neither on the necessary nor the useful, but principally on the very highest human goods: the contemplative knowledge of being and the good, and the understanding and worship of God. In both traditions, free lives, free studies, and free citizenship were available only for the few.

An important factor in the famous quarrel between the Ancients and the Moderns concerns the question of freedom. Is genuine freedom only for the few, or for all human beings? And if we say "all," do we mean human beings everywhere, no matter their race, gender, or cultural background? Modern European liberalism ostensibly supports freedom for everyone.[15] But modern liberalism is an historically developing tradition that takes different forms in different countries at different times. It originally begins in Great Britain in the seventeenth century with John Locke's defense of the natural human rights to life, liberty, and property. It later expands into Adam Smith's defense of economic liberalism (*laissez-faire*) in the *Wealth of Nations*. Only to be partly modified and adjusted by John Stuart Mill's account of *utility* in *On Liberty*.

But there are also distinct and important liberal traditions in France (Montesquieu, Constant, and de Tocqueville). In Germany (Kant, Herder, Hegel, and Von Humboldt). And in the United States, with the emergence of Utilitarian and Expressive Individualism during the nineteenth century.[16] In its original British form, the moral, political, and economic ontology of liberalism is atomistic. Human beings are characterized as "punctual selves," enjoying natural rights, but without corresponding civic obligations. This early British liberalism also shares the Enlightenment's skepticism of the Roman Trinity, the medieval reliance on religion, tradition, and authority as the stable foundations of a good society. Liberalism distrusts authority and the inherited hierarchies on which it depends. It pictures self-governing communities as originating in a voluntary social contract in which rights bearing individuals freely consent to limited government in accordance with self-imposed rules. And unlike the Roman Trinity, it looks to future progress, scientific, technological and economic, rather than inherited wisdom, as the basis of a just community.

In its original conception of freedom, liberalism has two complementary dimensions: negative liberty, meaning *freedom from* the governing authority of others; and positive liberty, meaning self-governing *autonomy* based on individual choice. But, over time, this overly simple picture of liberty and community was critically modified in response to very important historical events. The overthrow of monarchy; the diminished authority and influence of the landed aristocracy; Napoleon's European imperialism with the dramatic rise of nationalism it provoked; the unregulated expansion of the Industrial Revolution and monopoly capitalism; brutal European imperialism in Asia and Africa; and the unprecedented threats to liberty and justice from totalitarian movements and regimes in the twentieth century.

Historical change, as it always does, brought progress and decline to the liberal tradition. It revealed the cultural and institutional limits of liberalism's atomistic anthropology, and the grave inadequacy of the restricted form of government liberalism originally favored. The provisional result has been a complex and evolving tradition that merits our criticism for its ontological and political prejudices, but also our respect for the civic goods it has helped to achieve and protect.[17]

Despite the significant weaknesses of liberal theory and practice, I openly acknowledge, together with Charles Taylor, the historical achievements of Western liberalism. These achievements constitute part of the enduring greatness of liberal democracies, and they stand as a rebuke to any one-sided or wholesale rejection of the modern liberal tradition.

1. Liberalism has historically defended religious toleration and freedom of worship and conscience.
2. It has forcefully defended intellectual liberty, unrestricted freedom of inquiry and expression, as essential conditions of personal and public development.

3. It helped to establish limited constitutional governments founded on the principles of subsidiarity and the separation of powers. On balance, liberals have been sensitive to the dangers of concentrated political power, but much less wary of economic monopolies and trusts, and their inordinate and controlling influence on democratic governments.
4. In principle, it insisted on the rule of law (not men) and the equal treatment of all citizens under the law.
5. It developed and articulated a bill of individual rights or legally secured civil and political liberties.
6. It effectively opposed the arbitrary reduction of personal choices and socio-economic opportunities due to race, gender, religion, and Socrates.
7. It affirmed the ethical importance of "ordinary life," of companionate marriage and the family, of productive and justly remunerated work, and of a broad range of social and cultural activities.
8. It encouraged the ideal of responsible personal freedom, but regularly neglected the intellectual, moral, and civic education that underlies and sustains authentic liberty. In opposing despotic authority and repressive orthodoxies, liberalism often unwisely rejected the validity of authority and hierarchy as such.
9. While encouraging the free expression of critical dissent, liberals often lapse into an adversarial suspicion of all forms of government and public authority.[18]

The great strength of liberalism has been its opposition to arbitrary and despotic power, and its support for secure individual rights. Its historic weakness has been its intellectual dependence on a reductive anthropology and sociology, the atomized conception of the unsituated punctual self, and an uncritical and inflated theory of human freedom. These endemic oversights have made it difficult for liberal societies to achieve an enduring and essential ethical balance that combines freedom with responsibility, liberty with justice, and individual rights with strong political and social obligations.

In chapter 4, "Effective Freedom: What it Is and Why it Matters," I seek to bring the insights and concerns of the opening chapters together. I focus particularly on the distinctive contribution of a genuine liberal education to the achievement of effective freedom, and the importance of effective freedom to a free, just, and inclusive democracy. As the chapter unfolds, I try to clarify what effective freedom is, how it is achieved, the different stages of human development on which it depends, and the critical role of liberal education in shaping informed and responsible citizens within a free, just, and pluralistic community.

Drawing on the insights of Bernard Lonergan, I argue that the differences identified in chapter 1 need not become partisan divisions, if all of our citizens receive a common education that fosters a shared knowledge of the world, a shared set of liberal arts and virtues, and a shared commitment to informed and responsible citizenship.[19] This common education begins at birth in each citizen's family, takes place in both schools and civil society, and culminates in the liberal education received in a well-designed college. But how that liberal education is conceived and implemented makes all the difference.

In America today, the nature and purpose of a college education are largely conceived in economic rather than political terms. College is seen primarily as a preparation for the competitive job market, as a means of advancing one's economic self-interest, and of gaining an economic advantage over one's civic peers. But this one-sided emphasis on the economic is at best a half truth. While nearly all democratic citizens must work for a living, and acquire the knowledge and skills that requires, the civic education a sound democracy demands is focused on the common good that its citizens must freely achieve together. As I argue later in chapter 7, a united and cooperative democracy, a free and self-governing community, deliberately puts the political before the economic, the common good before self-interest, and the liberal arts and virtues before the specialized skills that bring economic success.

A second source of confusion about liberal education involves neglecting the difference between education and learning. Between the common knowledge essential to informed and cooperative citizenship, and the specialized learning on which the modern university is based. Unlike research universities, properly focused on advancing specialized knowledge, the liberal arts college is the last serious cultural institution we have that treats its students and faculty as citizens of an intellectual, cultural, and political community, and expects them to achieve the shared knowledge, arts, and virtues such an effective community requires.

But preparing our students for responsible citizenship means seeing them as members of an historically situated community. A community where the common fund of knowledge enlarges over time, where the shared historical narratives are revised to correct earlier oversights and prejudices, and where excluded models of cultural excellence are finally given their due recognition and praise. The governing spirit of a thriving democracy and of the shared liberal education on which it depends is one of openness and engaged pluralism. A spirit committed to the quest for comprehensive understanding and justice, rather than the hunger for intellectual certainty and emotional security.[20]

Because historical change brings both progress and decline, cultural and institutional, and because it requires finite and fallible citizens to discern together how best to respond to the new and unfamiliar, it is essential that they trust and respect each other. That their dialogues are based on factual truths, a critical sensitivity to bias in its different forms, a shared sense of values that is open-ended and revisable, and a deep respect for the "other" that enables strangers eventually to become friends and fellow citizens. It is no accident that, even with the best intentions, historical democracies have failed to fulfill their highest aspirations and ideals. "Liberty and justice for all" requires the effective freedom of each adult citizen, and the humility, generosity and practical wisdom of the interactive communities to which they belong. The barriers to a just and inclusive democracy are clearly deep-rooted and enduring.[21]

In chapter 5, "The Critical Appropriation of Traditions: Reflections of a Teacher," I reflect further on the three elements of the educational trinity: (1) Dedicated teachers who know, love, and accept responsibility for the world and the young; (2) Maturing students, open to learning from their teachers the common fund of knowledge, factual and evaluative, that adult life will require them to exercise as citizens; and (3) A historically revisable curriculum, based on the critical appropriation, by both teachers and students, of the different historical traditions that have shaped our democratic institutions and practices. I then argue that this critical educational process is particularly difficult now in the light of what I call "The Modern Predicament."[22]

I begin the argument by clarifying the modern cultural predicament, and the specific challenges, personal, cultural, and institutional, that it creates for civic education. And I conclude it by proposing how best to respond to these challenges with humility and wisdom. To understand "the predicament," we need to focus carefully on three essential features of the distinctively modern outlook. Its unprecedented moral aspirations, historical consciousness, and passion for criticism. Those moral aspirations can be found in the revolutionary ideal of liberty, equality, and fraternity for all human beings, whoever they are and wherever they may live.

But while the ideal remains compelling, our understanding of its components needs to be clarified in the light of human nature and the human condition. The ideal of liberty, for historically situated and developing human beings, is best understood as effective freedom rather than unlimited subjective autonomy. A critical account of human equality must be formed in the light of personal development, a complex educational process that begins at birth and unfolds gradually and by stages into adulthood. A process in which the effective authority of adults is essential to cultivating the effective freedom of their young pupils. And a credible account of fraternity, in which all human beings share genuine care and concern for each other, depends on strong moral sources that modernity's critical passions often seek to discredit. In the words of Charles Taylor, the very high moral standards of Modernity require equally strong moral sources (God, nature, the unrestricted intellectual and moral aspirations of each human person) if they are to be genuinely achieved.[23]

The historical consciousness of the West greatly expanded in the nineteenth and twentieth centuries. Through study, trade, colonization, and the development of the human sciences, both teachers and their students became aware of different cultural traditions and practices. And through global patterns of immigration, commerce, and travel, the remote and "far off" was regularly brought near. In this way, we learned that our political, religious, economic, and educational practices often differ significantly from those of others. But the experience of pluralism problematizes. It makes fair-minded people wonder whether their ways of doing things, and the cultural convictions and values they transmit to their young, are merely inherited prejudices that cannot bear critical scrutiny. However, if this heightened cultural pluralism is not to dissolve into cultural relativism, then historically minded teachers must discover a fair and non-biased way forward. To put our common dilemma bluntly, what does "critical belonging" to our historically minded democratic communities require of both teachers and students today?

The third defining aspect of Modernity are its severe critical passions. Beginning with Descartes' demand for hyperbolic doubt in his scientific quest for certainty; followed by Kant's insistence on "pure practical reason" in the moral realm; then the "subversive genealogies" of Marx, Nietzsche, and Freud whom Paul Ricoeur dubbed "the masters of suspicion"; culminating in the post-modern critique of scientific objectivity and truth. The cumulative result of these powerful critical initiatives is a pervasive culture of suspicion that effectively discredits the strong moral sources and normative standards a free and just democracy requires.

If this cultural analysis is sound, the defining elements of the "Modern Predicament" are mutually incompatible. But what, then, are contemporary teachers and students to do? They can't credibly revert to a state of pre-modern innocence before the advent of modern doubt and suspicion. Nor, can they legitimately endorse the celebrated "genealogies of suspicion" whose discrediting claims are inconsistent with the normative cognitive processes that supposedly justify them.

What I propose, by contrast, is defending the intellectual and moral ideal of self-transcendence, both personal and communal; clarifying the normative processes through which intellectual and moral self-transcendence are achieved; identifying the operative biases that regularly prevent its achievement; and explicitly criticizing the prominent ideologies used to justify bias in its numerous and powerful forms. Only if teachers and students commit to this demanding and continuous dialectic can their "critical appropriation of our historical traditions," ancient, modern, and post-modern, hope to succeed. Enabling us to preserve and transmit the best of our complex and uneven cultural heritage.[24]

Chapter 6 is entitled "Democracy in America: The Sources of our Discontent." Writing this book in a time of democratic crisis, I was constantly aware of reenacting an important pattern in American history. I was inspired, in particular, by the enduring work of Alexis de Tocqueville nearly two hundred years ago. Tocqueville, an aristocratic French citizen, had visited the United States for nine months in the early 1830s. The enduring fruits of his visit appeared several years later (1835,1840) in two great works of political reflection and criticism, *Democracy in America*, Volumes I and II. Together, they set a standard for sympathetic and unsparing democratic criticism. "Men will not receive the truth from their enemies; and it is very seldom offered to them by their friends." *Democracy in America*, Volume II.

Having witnessed the revolution in France devolve into terror, Napoleonic despotism, and monarchical restoration, Tocqueville was particularly sensitive to the struggle for democratic liberty, and the sources of democratic despotism. In Volume I of *Democracy in America*, he focused on the uneven political effects of democratic equality; and in Volume II on the cultural influence of equality on the minds and hearts of American citizens. A devoted friend of both liberty and justice, Tocqueville memorably articulated the causes and effects of democratic despotism: an over reliance on centralized government; the weakening of the voluntary associations that constitute civil society, which Tocqueville called "the grammar schools of liberty"; and a retreat by ordinary citizens into the narrow confines of their private lives (democratic individualism). For Tocqueville, the convergence of these causes threatened both the personal and political liberty of American citizens. But he insisted that this despotic result was not inevitable. To prevent it, he called for a new science of republican politics based on the following principles: vigorous and pervasive township government; decentralized public administration based on the principle of subsidiarity; vital and active voluntary associations; the impartial rule of law administered by an independent judiciary; a free, independent and responsible press; a community of well-informed citizens committed to liberty and justice at all levels of American society.[25]

Though many of Tocqueville's insights remain important and valid, and he continues to serve as a model of sympathetic democratic criticism, the two hundred years since his sojourn in America have brought dramatic changes to our country's population, institutions, and culture. And with them, new sources of democratic discontent, and new reflections on the state of our democracy. Among the recent critics from whom I have learned the most are: Hannah Arendt, E.J. Dionne, Norman Ornstein, Thomas Mann, Charles Taylor, Michael Sandel, and William Galston. In the second half of chapter 6, I focus especially on Galston's forceful account of our democratic discontents.[26]

Galston believes that our present political crisis has arisen because a transformative period in American political life has come to an end. He is referring to the Progressive era in American politics, initiated and sustained by Theodore and Franklin Roosevelt. A sixty-year period of active, problem-solving government and pragmatic social reform. A period culminating in FDR's New Deal and Lyndon Johnson's Great Society. But the national movement for civil rights, the demoralizing defeat in Vietnam, the counter-cultural excesses of the 1960s and 70s, the weakening of the American labor movement, and the oil shocks and hyper-inflation of the 1970s converged to end the great Progressive era and to begin the new era of Ronald Reagan's nostalgic conservatism.

Stepping back from the bitter partisan struggle between progressives and conservatives, Galston identifies three powerful sources of division within American democracy today: economic anxiety and insecurity; cultural fragmentation (the loss of a cohesive civic community); and a broad decline in public confidence in our political and cultural institutions. I shall include here a very brief overview of Galston's critical analysis.[27]

At the root of our national economic anxiety is an historic transformation in the American economy. The dynamic and continuous technological revolution, the competitive challenges of globalization, heightened sensitivity to the environmental dangers of unregulated growth, the deepening threat of global warming to the entire planet, and the marked decline in necessary public investment and support have created a nest of intractable problems for democratic policy makers, planners, and citizens. The cumulative effect has been a dramatic increase in social and economic inequality and insecurity, and a marked shift in political power to the most wealthy and influential members of American society. But our political response to these grave and mounting challenges has been anemic. Why? Because we lack a national political consensus on how to address them effectively. An exemplary case of special interests and minority power taking precedence over the common good.

A second important source of democratic unrest is the decline in America's civil society, the intermediary associations that mediate between the power of government and the profit driven transactions of the economic marketplace. As Tocqueville wisely emphasized, these voluntary associations, political, religious, intellectual, cultural, and educational, play an indispensable role in creating a unified, engaged, and responsible democratic citizenry. Their communal spirit checks the democratic tendency to narrow self-interest and the democratic passions for material prosperity and comfort. It is within civil society that ordinary men and women become responsible citizens; that they learn to know, love, and act on behalf of the entire community.

Galston agrees with Robert Putnam and Charles Taylor that American civil society and the principal sources of civic education are showing serious signs of decline.[28] Marriages and families are weaker; neighborhoods less cohesive; schools provide very uneven and imperfect educations; the university's moral and civic authority has markedly declined; the public media have become increasingly shrill and profit driven; and the traditional civic associations are losing members and influence. As Tocqueville predicted, when these voluntary associations weaken, the focus of ordinary citizens turns inward. Too many of us lack reliable knowledge of worldly realities and sources of division, relevant historical contexts, recurrent patterns of injustice, and dangerous concentrations of power.[29] Without this shared knowledge, we become easily manipulated by propaganda, scapegoating, and deliberate misinformation and lies. When our attention is drawn to politics, it is often orchestrated campaigns of resentment and grievance that capture our attention and loyalty.

Galston's third critical theme is the steady erosion of political authority. An erosion caused by the loss of governmental independence, impartiality, and effectiveness. Most Americans now believe that our country is governed for the benefit of a wealthy, influential, and self-serving minority.[30] This troubling conviction of oligarchic despotism has had a demoralizing effect on our entire public life. It has weakened public confidence in democratic government; generated contempt for public officials and institutions; and significantly reduced the informed and responsible conduct of ordinary citizens. Tocqueville's grave warnings about "democratic individualism" and "democratic despotism" retain special force at this time, making a profound renewal of civic education both urgent and inescapable. But where should such a renewal begin and what critical reforms must it emphasize?

In responding to this challenge, I seek to combine the strategy of "critical retrieval" with that of "critical dismantling." Their deliberate combination serves as the core of chapter 7, "The Cultural Struggle for American Democracy."

What does it mean to be an American citizen today? And why have so many Americans become distrustful of government, suspicious of politics, and uncertain of their civic obligations? For me, these questions are fundamentally cultural. The aim of chapter 7 is to clarify the profound civic implications of important cultural changes within American democracy over the last two hundred and fifty years. In my judgment, the most powerful forces at work in our society today are anti-political. If we agree with Charles Taylor, that a healthy democracy requires creating a never stable balance between political and economic concerns, between the democratic struggle for equal liberty and justice and the capitalist struggle for profit and financial security, then how did the acquisitive spirit of capitalism become so deeply entrenched in American public life that the traditional authority of politics over economics was almost completely reversed?

To answer that question credibly, I deliberately contrast the civic republican account of politics, "The lost treasure of the American Revolution" (Arendt) with the "Imperial assumptions of economics."[31] What are the basic principles of civic republicanism? (1) *Civic Virtue*, which means consistently putting the common good before the private interests of individuals and groups; (2) *Political Liberty*, which means regular, active, and informed participation by adult citizens in the common project of republican self-government; and (3) *Public Happiness*, which means the shared enjoyment and significance ordinary citizens discover in their responsible conduct of public affairs. These complementary principles are essential to the political convictions and actions of the founding generation that created our constitutional and democratic republic.[32]

But according to Arendt and Robert Bellah (*Habits of the Heart*), they were neglected, forgotten, or deliberately rejected during the long nineteenth century, so that an especially valuable part of our American political inheritance remains unknown and without strong cultural influence today. If the core elements of civic republicanism (love of the world and the distinctive joys of responsible citizenship; the recognized dignity of free speech, deliberative reasoning, and shared decision making; the intrinsic value of political agents, events and communities; and the singular treasure of public liberty) are a significant part of our cultural heritage, then how did they come to be widely neglected or forgotten? In the second half of chapter 7, I focus on the reductive economic convictions that largely account for this grave cultural and institutional loss.[33]

Economic practice and theory deeply informed the cultural outlook of Western modernity. By the nineteenth century, a radical set of assumptions about human existence became widely accepted in "enlightened circles." I refer to these reductive anthropological prejudices as "the imperial assumptions of economics." What are these assumptions, and what has been their unwelcome effect on the American understanding of education, politics, and citizenship?

(1) The true basis of all human association is economic, serving the preservation and extension of individual and species life; (2) The underlying motive of all human activity is self-interest, so that normative appeals to disinterested and principled activity are either hypocritical or naïve; (3) All human activities are to be measured and appraised in terms of their productive potential, the "fruits and works" they are able consistently to produce; (4) Leisure is no longer the basis of "culture," of the intrinsically liberal activities in which human beings are free to engage. But simply the temporary suspension of productive labor that creates time for entertainment and play; and (5) The cultural revision of "noblesse oblige." Throughout Western history, the dominant economic class had always assumed the obligations of political leadership.

But the rise of the bourgeoisie in the eighteenth and nineteenth centuries was marked by explicitly anti-political prejudices. Merchants, bankers, industrialists, and traders insisted on "freedom from" government interference and regulation, so that they could actively pursue economic gain. What the bourgeoisie demanded from government was security: the protection of their lives, family, property and investments, with the confidence that unimpeded economic activity (*laissez-faire*) would insure the well-being of all.

In this historic cultural reversal, first politics became subordinated to economics, the deliberative assembly to the capitalist marketplace. Then politics was transformed into another form of business, democratic citizens into active consumers, political speech into public relations, and reasoned deliberation into emotional bumper stickers intended to manipulate unreflective emotions, rather than to inform and persuade thoughtful minds. While political critics and commentators became fascinated by the fierce competition for market share, mindlessly reporting who's winning and losing in the endless struggle for political influence and power.[34]

Can the reductive grip of these one-sided cultural and political prejudices be broken? Can American democracy recover its original and energizing civic republican spirit? The deepest reforms we require today are intellectual, moral, and cultural. At every level of our divided society, we need to reexamine the way we think, speak, and feel about education, citizenship, government, and the human good. We have created a public culture that emphasizes individual rights and neglects public responsibilities; that celebrates the pursuit of self-interest and casts doubt on the great civic virtues; that highlights individual misconduct and glosses over systemic injustice; and that encourages skeptical distrust and suspicion of the collaborative discovery and achievement of the common good. As a reflective and responsible citizen, I deliberately wrote this book, with its interwoven layers of argument, to reverse these anti-political prejudices, and to renew our commitment to the cultural convictions that originally inspired our democracy.[35]

Thinking about the nature and purpose of education forces us to examine permanent philosophical concerns about human nature, the human condition, human development, human knowledge, and the human good. In chapter 8, "Our Search for Wisdom: The Stories We Live By," I reflect on these enduring concerns in the light of three influential narratives about human well-being.

I begin chapter 8 by summarizing the central argument of this book: Our common need for education, especially liberal education, to cultivate the excellences that a democratic community requires in order to flourish (actively seeking liberty and justice for all its citizens). But I recognize that contrasting views of human nature and the human condition express themselves in conflicting stories about human freedom and the human good. I then review

three of the most influential stories that have shaped our educational practices
and aspirations.

Protagoras's account of our difficult human origins, and of the skills we
require (technical and rhetorical) to offset our natural deficiencies. Rousseau's
account in his *Second Discourse on the Origin of Inequality* of the original
freedom, happiness, and goodness of human beings in the state of nature.
A well-being achieved, according to Rousseau, without education and con-
certed community effort. And most impressively, Plato's myth of the cave in
Republic VII, in which the human need for *metanoia*, intellectual and moral
conversion, plays the central role in the human achievement of justice.[36]

I then examine an important ambiguity in Plato's memorable story, a story
modeled in critical respects on the personal history of Socrates of Athens.
Like Socrates, the liberated prisoner in the cave gradually discovers his original ignorance of what is real and good. Then, after painfully leaving the cave
and entering the light, the prisoner slowly discovers the intelligible forms of
being and the ultimate form of the Good (mythically symbolized by the sun).
Delighted by these discoveries, the prisoner desires to remain in the light,
but is forced by his liberators (his anonymous teachers) to return to the cave,
so that he may share these remarkable discoveries with his civic peers. His
goal is to liberate them from the bondage of ignorance they originally shared,
and to lead them, through their own conversions, to a personal knowledge
of the good.

But strikingly, Socrates himself never claimed to be wise. He called himself
a *philosopher,* a lover of wisdom, who longed for an excellence he recognized
he did not possess. And he summoned his fellow citizens to join him in the
quest for wisdom, knowing its singular importance and its troubling absence
from their common life. What then is the relevance of this striking ambiguity, between the secure *possession of* and the dedicated *quest for* wisdom, for
our account of liberal education and responsible democratic citizenship.[37]If
liberal education cannot make us wise, with a definitive knowledge of being
and the good, what excellences can it develop in the personal and public lives
of informed and responsible citizens?

It can lead us, as in the cave story, to recognize our ignorance, our lack of
definitive knowledge of what is real and good. It can also heighten our longing (our *eros*) for the arts and virtues we need to discover and achieve the
common good together. It can effectively cultivate the virtues of self-control
and courage, of humility and patience, of critical belonging and forgiveness
that all citizens need to fulfill their civic obligations. And it can articulate the
norms of collaborative dialogue and decision-making that enable finite and
fallible citizens to achieve liberty and justice together.

To confirm these classical insights, I conclude the chapter with a final
story, John Dunne's *Parable of the Mountain,* that reveals how the surprising

personal discoveries gained on the mountain top can lead us freely to return to the valley that we share with the whole human race.[38] Not forced to return, as in the *Republic*, but because we're inspired by a deeper understanding of God and God's goodness that only climbing the mountain makes possible.

In the concluding chapter, "Our Common Struggle with Unwelcome Truths," I explicitly recall several significant dangers that we face as American citizens: political, cultural, religious, and intellectual. Then I reflect on how we can address these challenges effectively in our own speech and conduct. Leading me to propose four essential imperatives intended to foster collaborative and fruitful dialogues across differences in belief, background and cultural, and political outlook.

1. Seek the fullness of truth in a spirit of humility and realism, clearly acknowledging the singular importance of factual and evaluative truth, and the finitude and fallibility of all human inquiry.
2. Speak the truth, as you now understand it, in a spirit of genuine friendship.
3. Share the common world that truth reveals in a spirit of cooperative solidarity.
4. Especially now, be particularly attentive and resistant to the demagogue's despotic reliance on available scapegoats.

Responding wisely and effectively to the many dangers threatening our democracy requires all of the virtues outlined in these four imperatives: humility, generosity, practical wisdom, critical realism and civic friendship. But sadly, we are not born with any of these virtues. They have to be actively cultivated by our common civic education from birth until we become mature citizens. For, without these essential virtues, we will regularly respond to unwelcome truths with denial, diversion, and the deliberate discrediting of those who tell us what we do not want to hear, accept, or live by.[39]

National cultural and spiritual unity does not require uniformity of opinion and judgment. But it does require the fruitful interaction and dialogue of the diverse groups within American society: women and men; young and old; religious and skeptical; traditional and innovative; affluent and poor; and the full range of racial and ethnic communities stretching from the Atlantic to the Pacific. *E pluribus unum* is the declaration of a sustained and responsible democratic process, not of a fixed and static result. The collaborative civic engagement of citizens in our pluralistic democracy is the only way to restore genuine and sustainable unity. But that engagement will not and cannot unite us, unless we foster, prize, and reliably exercise the essential virtues of a liberal and democratic education.

NOTES

1. The continuing tension between America's founding principles, clearly articulated in the Declaration of Independence, and their legal enactment in the Constitution, has been present since the creation of the republic. Subsequent amendments to the Constitution have only partly redressed this enduring tension.

2. The assassination of President Lincoln clearly altered the tone and character of post-war Reconstruction. But the barriers to racial justice were deep and formidable, regardless of who led the nation after the Civil War.

3. Johnson, in fact, sought to combine both racial and economic justice simultaneously. But the divisive tensions of the 1960s made this critical combination exceedingly difficult.

4. The enduring power of the isolationist strain in American history is clearly reflected in Donald Trump's populist call for "America First."

5. As the forms of American pluralism have increased, so has our need for a comprehensive civic education.

6. The conservative Republican party that Ronald Reagan created no longer exists in its original form. The party now loyal to Donald Trump is more populist, more isolationist, more demagogic, and rhetorically less hopeful than its immediate predecessor.

7. The national and global challenges we face in the twenty-first century would be difficult for any democratic government to master. But a divided nation, unable to agree on its most important challenges, is singularly compromised by its internal divisions.

8. While the different American communities and institutions play different roles in achieving the common good, they all require the civic virtues cultivated by a liberal education to execute these roles effectively, especially in times of crisis.

9. Though I have benefitted greatly from reading all these authors, I have consistently approached them in the spirit of Aristotle. "All our predecessors render us the double service of revealing the truth, or missing the mark, thus challenging us to get to the root of the matter ourselves." *De Anima* 403 b 22.

10. I have taken as the defining aim of American democracy "Liberty and Justice for all our citizens." But to clarify this aim in the light of our troubled history and the specific crises we presently face requires distinguishing "effective freedom" from other limited understandings of liberty; as well as showing the dependence of comprehensive justice on the virtues "effective freedom" entails.

11. I first encountered the distinction between education and learning in Hannah Arendt's essay, "The Crisis of Education" in her remarkable collection *Between Past and Future*.

12. A liberal education at the level of our time requires close attention to both constants and variables, particularly in shaping the college's curriculum. These periodic revisions reflect both changes in scientific and historical knowledge, as well as the discovery of models of excellence previously unknown or unappreciated. These models can be found in all of the creative arts, including literature, music, painting, sculpture, dance, architecture, and theatre.

13. For a vivid account of the several forms of bias and their negative effects on human cognition, see Bernard Lonergan, *Insight*.

14. Chapter 2 is a highly revised version of a Convocation address I gave at Vassar while I was still teaching there.

15. While the Moderns deliberately expand the scope of freedom, they also tend to narrow its ethical and political import.

16. For Robert Bellah's clarifying account of Utilitarian and Expressive Individualism, see *Habits of the Heart*.

17. A very good example of the "critical appropriation of traditions" referred to in Chapter 5.

18. See Taylor's *Sources of the Self* and also *A Secular Age*. Two works that have deeply shaped my thinking in this book.

19. I rely greatly on Lonergan's *Insight* and *Method in Theology* throughout this chapter on effective freedom.

20. The important contrast between "the quest for unrestricted understanding" and "the quest for certainty," between a mind and heart open to change and a spirit committed to reassuring certainties, is a recurrent and critical theme throughout this book.

21. This difficulty has always been true for democracies, but it is especially true in a pluralistic, continental democracy like our own in the twenty-first century.

22. I borrow freely from Michael Polanyi's *Personal Knowledge* throughout this chapter.

23. All three of these themes, effective freedom, historically situated subjectivity, and moral sources capable of self-transcendence, serve as the philosophical core of this work.

24. See *Authenticity As Self-Transcendence: The Enduring Insights of Bernard Lonergan* by Michael McCarthy.

25. Tocqueville here develops and amplifies Montesquieu's account of republican government in *The Spirit of the Laws*.

26. Galston's account can be found in *Debating Democracy's Discontents*, Anita Allen and Milton Regan, editors, New York, Oxford University Press, 1998.

27. I seek to distinguish clearly between Galston's trenchant analysis of our discontents and the concrete remedies that he proposes to resolve them.

28. See, in particular, Robert Putnam's *Bowling Alone* and Charles Taylor's *The Ethics of Authenticity*.

29. This is the type of background knowledge that a free and responsible press would regularly and reliably communicate to informed citizens.

30. Two different forms of elitism are the focus of popular discontent. An elitism of the wealthy that dominates national economic policy on taxation and regulation in particular. And an elitism of the college educated that dominates our public culture and educational policy. For a critique of "educational elitism," see Michael Sandel's *The Tyranny of Merit*.

31. See the final chapter in Arendt's important work, *On Revolution*, New York, Viking Press, 1963.

32. See Joseph Ellis, *American Dialogue*, New York, Viking Press, 2018.

33. The following is a composite account that draws on many historical sources, especially *The Worldly Philosophers* by Robert Heilbroner, New York, Simon and Schuster, 1986.

34. This helps to explain why contemporary political "analysis" is focused on the interpretation of "opinion polls," rather than an appraisal of the objective merits of public policy proposals. Do they really contribute to the common good, and what are the existing barriers to their enactment?

35. My genuine belief is that without this renewal our democratic crisis will only become more severe and intractable.

36. Though I have reservations about Plato as a political and educational theorist, I fully endorse his emphasis on *metanoia*, intellectual and moral conversion, in both of these correlated fields.

37. Another instance of the important contrast between "the quest for certainty" and the "quest for comprehensive understanding."

38. A parable drawn from Dunne's remarkable work, *The Way of All the Earth*, Notre Dame, University of Notre Dame Press, 1978.

39. I am reminded here of the enduring biblical warning, "A prophet is without honor in his own country" (Mark, 6:4).

Chapter 1

"A House Divided Against Itself Cannot Stand"

The contemporary United States is a deeply divided country, with many sources, areas, and levels of division.[1] Divisions about racial, ethnic, and gender equality. What does genuinely equal citizenship require for native Americans, African Americans, non-European immigrants, and women? And what are the appropriate roles for education, government, and civil society in achieving and protecting full and equal citizenship for all Americans today?

Regional divisions in customs, traditions, beliefs, and cultural and political priorities between citizens living in rural areas and small towns, and citizens living in major urban areas and the suburbs that surround them. Can the same set of public policies effectively address the legitimate concerns and challenges facing these very different American communities?

Educational, cultural, and political disparities between citizens graduating from American colleges and universities, and citizens whose formal education ended in high school. What common forms of education are needed to prepare all citizens for the rights and responsibilities of democratic citizenship today?

Economic and social divisions between those who have far more than they need, and the many individuals and families living in poverty or suffering severe deprivation and insecurity. What are the principal causes of social and economic inequality in America, and what degree of inequality makes a just and unified democracy unachievable?

Religious divisions between traditionalists and fundamentalists, and genuine believers of different faiths (or of no faith) who accept the discoveries of empirical science, the arts and virtues cultivated by liberal education, the norms and principles of constitutional democracy, and a multilateral foreign policy with an evolving set of global alliances. What are the cultural and political implications for American democracy of living in an increasingly secular society.[2]

Generational divisions among Americans born before and after 1980. Divisions in their level of trust in political leaders, parties, and institutions. Their contrasting appraisals of American history and American justice. Their specific ways of learning about the world, and the different teachers whom they admire and respect. How successful are our educational and cultural practices in developing genuine community and collaborative trust and dialogue among our old and young citizens?

Finally, critical differences in the sources of information, analysis and appraisal on which American citizens rely to make sense of the complex world that we share. What are the enduring effects on public discourse and deliberation of systemic lying, constant disinformation, and the deliberate cultivation of mistrust and suspicion for partisan purposes? When the divisive cognitive and political effects of individual and group bias become widely accepted in a democratic society, can we still reasonably aspire to discovering and achieving the common good together?[3]

These important divisions and others make it difficult for Americans to agree on the major challenges confronting our country, and on the best ways to meet them as a highly diverse but potentially unified people.

What are some of the most prominent challenges we presently face? Climate change and the related environmental, economic, and energy policies, local, national, and global, that are needed to address it responsibly. Creating a wise, fair, trusted, and effective public health system, both at home and abroad. Significant voter suppression, partisan gerrymandering, dark money, and deliberately cultivated distrust and suspicion that threaten electoral integrity and personal safety at all levels of government and politics. The scandal of constant gun violence and repeated and deadly mass shootings throughout our country. Our need for just and comprehensive immigration reform, a need that will only deepen with the corrosive and destabilizing effects of global warming and regional violence. Our glaring lack of bipartisan agreement on the appropriate role of the federal government in achieving security, liberty, and justice for all our citizens. The legitimate but limited role of diverse religious beliefs and practices in shaping public life and indirectly influencing public policy and law. Accurately identifying our allies and adversaries, foreign and domestic, in forging and enacting wise and well-supported public policies. Effectively educating all young Americans for the rights and responsibilities of citizenship. Responding wisely and fairly to the merits and limitations of major technological developments and the uneven economic and social consequences of international trade.[4]

One reason these national challenges are now so acute and divisive is the lack of agreement among our citizens, and our major political parties, about our troubled national history, but especially the history of America after World War II. For a shared understanding and appraisal of our common past is essential to acknowledging and wisely responding to our existing divisions and challenges. Some important areas of historical disagreement include:

Civil rights: the unfinished and still divisive effort to achieve genuine racial equality and desegregation in our schools, neighborhoods, social and economic institutions, and positions of political leadership.

Have native Americans, black Americans, Asian and Latin Americans achieved genuinely equal citizenship and opportunity in contemporary America? And if they have not, what are the political, cultural, institutional, and personal barriers preventing them from doing so?

Full equality for women: the continuing struggle of American women to achieve full equality with men in education, law, employment opportunities, compensation, and in securing well-deserved positions of leadership and authority, domestic, religious, cultural, and political.

Federalism, subsidiarity, and the common good: what is the appropriate role of government, federal, state, and local, in promoting social and economic justice and true political liberty and equality? Opposing answers to this question often rely on fundamentally different appraisals of the New Deal, the Great Society, and the unregulated market capitalism advocated by Ronald Reagan and *laissez-faire* economic conservatives. Since Reagan's presidency, however, open hostility to the federal government has only intensified. This hostility now extends to the government's role in fiscal and monetary policy, economic and environmental regulations, health care and health insurance, gun control, support for higher education, and nearly all aspects of our national safety net. Open espousals of libertarian ideology and the traditional Southern insistence on "state sovereignty" have led to both implicit and explicit rejections of America's common good as the proper aim of genuine political activity. In a viable federalism, political power and authority are allocated in proportion to demonstrated competence and need (the principle of subsidiarity). But where a smaller unit of power lacks the resources, knowledge, ability, and commitment to address effectively a genuinely national problem or challenge, then the higher unit of authority must act. Justly exercising subsidiarity requires shared experience and practical wisdom, not ideological bias and partisan rigidity.[5]

Foreign policy and our critical alliances throughout the globe: We have largely maintained our critical post-war alliances in Europe (NATO and the European Union) and Asia (Japan, South Korea, Australia) even after the end of the Cold War and the rise of international terrorism. But these alliances are now less secure, given Donald Trump's unilateralism (his crude insistence on "America First") and his still dominant influence on much of the Republican party. And the heightened political instability in the United States makes it unclear how long these important and stabilizing alliances will survive. Though we commonly distrust China, Putin's Russia, Iran, and North Korea, for example, we are still struggling to create a post-Cold War foreign policy consensus on international security, global trade, climate change, equitable taxation, immigration, terrorism, political Islam, Ukraine, and the disappointing results of the Arab Spring. This lack of consensus also extends to our working relations with Mexico and the fragile democracies of South America, Africa, and Asia, the best balance between hard and soft power in foreign affairs, and the strength and integrity of our departments of State and Defense. Were Trump, or a like-minded ally, to be re-elected, it's truly frightening to consider how much damage he and his administration would continue to inflict on our public institutions and traditional global alliances.[6]

As a self-governing democracy, we also suffer from mounting disagreement on reliable and trustworthy sources of information and institutional and cultural analysis. Some of this disagreement, when civil and evidence based, is healthy, but much of it is not. What is very unhealthy is deliberately cultivated distrust of the sciences and critical history, well-established media like Public Broadcasting and the *New York Times*, the higher education students receive at American colleges and universities, the integrity of government agencies like the IRS, the EPA, HEW, the Departments of Justice, Education, Labor and Energy by the political right and their media allies. Through denial, discrediting, outright lying and fear mongering, Fox News, Breitbart, One American News, Rush Limbaugh, Tucker Carlson, Steve Bannon, and other conspiracy minded commentators deliberately cultivate suspicion and conflict among our citizens in order to secure greater political power for themselves and their partisan supporters. Historically, this is the strategy of despots and their unprincipled enablers, not of informed and public-spirited citizens.[7]

Opposing trends: the parallel growth of inter-faith cooperation and zealous religious nationalism. In the decades after World War II, the historic American antagonism among Catholics, Protestants, and Jews largely subsided. There was a marked increase in interfaith cooperation, especially in support of economic, racial, and social justice; and a significant increase in intermarriage and friendships as well.

But a continuing decline in the percentage of practicing Catholics and mainline Protestants coincided with a marked rise in "evangelical communities," whose largely conservative appeal is both political and cultural. And the unchecked growth of political extremism has seen the recurrence of open and defiant anti-Semitism and Islamophobia, especially in the era of Trump. Finally, deepening divisions within Christian communities on matters of personal and public morality have fostered an intolerant Christian nationalism, modeled on Victor Orban's illiberal autocracy in Hungary. These serious cultural and political divisions, coupled with the Federalist Society's deepening influence on judicial appointments, have gravely weakened trust in the independence and impartiality of the judiciary, federal and state, but especially in the present Supreme Court. The court's recent decisions on abortion, gun regulations, religious liberty, affirmative action, and the government's regulatory authority have only heightened sectarian divisions within America.[8]

The state of our two major political parties, Democratic and Republican: In the 1950s, the Democrats were still largely united within the New Deal coalition: labor unions, much of the working class, Catholics, white Southerners, the great majority of teachers and scholars. Two important movements in the 1960s led to the collapse of that coalition: the insistence on full civil rights for African Americans and women, and the passionate national opposition to the Vietnam War.

Since that collapse, the Democratic party is still struggling to create a new and effective national coalition without the support of white Southerners, major portions of the white working class, and those who've embraced the moral, political and cultural priorities of the "religious right."[9]

Since the upheavals of 1968, the national electorate has become increasingly divided: between women (D) and men (R), between urban and suburban voters (D) and those in rural communities and small cities (R), between college educated (D) and high school educated citizens (R), between those who accept a more secular and diverse American society (D) and religious and social conservatives who do not (R). Between those who respect the results of scientific inquiry and their practical relevance for issues like climate change, public health, and gun control (D), and those who distrust science, governmental institutions, colleges and universities, and the principal media sources of shared information and analysis (R). Finally, the deep partisan divide between those who endorse a major role for the federal government in both domestic and foreign affairs (D), and those who stigmatize such a role as "Socialism or Marxism" (R).

In largely accepting Reagan's anti-government rhetoric and ideology, the contemporary Republican party has essentially abandoned the goals of economic and racial justice for all citizens. But things have only worsened since the election of President Obama, with the rise of the Tea Party and the Birther conspiracy, reaching their nadir with the electoral embrace of Donald Trump, an irresponsible lying narcissist, completely unfit for public office and national leadership. Sadly, the fierce partisan divide, in its several crippling forms, only serves to deepen the national divisions we have been seeking to understand and unravel.[10]

If this sobering analysis is accurate, it raises an inescapable question for our democracy. Do we have the internal resources, personal, moral, cultural, and political, to heal our numerous divisions and respond to our major challenges cooperatively and well? In short, does the democracy we presently have correspond to the democracy we urgently need?

At the personal level: How do most American citizens now see themselves and their civic responsibilities to our country and the world? Do they strive to be accurately informed about the state of our nation, and of the world that we share with others? To subordinate their individual and group interests to the common good, the comprehensive and enduring good of America as a whole? And to fulfill their fiduciary obligations to posterity: leaving all our descendants a livable planet, healthy democratic institutions, a just economy, a well-ordered world, and educational and cultural communities equal to the challenges of the present and future?[11]

At the cultural level: How well do we as a country prepare our young citizens for meeting their civic obligations? Through the practical example given by parents and peers to the young? Through the clarity, honesty, and depth of American education from elementary school through college? Through the one-sided focus of our public culture on greed, celebrity, and personal ambition? Through the decline of strong and credible religious communities dedicated to equal liberty and justice for all citizens? Through pervasive intellectual confusion about the meaning of responsible freedom, the dual importance of personal and communal responsibility, the priority of the common good over individual and group interests, and our common need for truth, fairness, humility, and integrity in all forms of human interaction and dialogue? Finally, the critical need for American businesses, corporations, and financial institutions to act responsibly and consistently for the public good?[12]

At the institutional level, how can we restore greater trust in and critical acceptance of our most important and essential public institutions? In marriage and the family; in our schools and the other sources of civic education; in credible and common sources of factual information and historical narrative; in the integrity and leadership of our political parties; in the independence and impartiality of our courts; in the equality and fairness of our criminal justice system; in the justice and integrity of our electoral practices, especially after Trump's Big Lie and its blind acceptance by so many of his ardent followers; in our shared sense of the fragility of democracies and of the personal, cultural, and institutional safeguards on which they rely?[13]

A free and just multi-racial society has eluded America since its origin. We clearly have made progress toward that high goal since our original war for independence. But that progress has consistently been followed by backlash and resistance, as it clearly is now. We still have important sources of national unity, factual and normative, but, it seems, even more powerful sources of division and paralysis. And the worst sources of our division are deliberately cultivated and exaggerated by demagogues to fracture our democracy and prevent us from achieving "liberty and justice for all."

Will we be wise, brave, humble, and generous enough to heal our deep wounds, overcome our resentments and fears, and freely cooperate as responsible citizens to achieve the American democracy we hope for and need? These are among the questions I seek to address in the interrelated chapters that follow.

All of them were written by a citizen and teacher, drawing on my long experience of this country, my careful study of its politically uneven history, and of the inescapable challenges it faces today. The leading idea I have followed is our common need as Americans for a much deeper and fuller understanding of freedom, personal and public. "High moral standards require strong moral sources." To articulate clearly those standards and sources, and the severe challenges they presently face, is my goal throughout this work.[14] Consistently living in accordance with those standards is our common obligation as citizens.

NOTES

1. The origins of the title phrase are biblical: Matthew 12:25; Mark 3:25. Abraham Lincoln also spoke these words to the legislature in Springfield, Illinois, before the Civil War.

2. See Charles Taylor's *A Secular Age* for three distinct but interrelated senses of the "secular." And my essay, "Toward a New Critical Center," *Method*, 1999, that carefully distinguishes Classicist consciousness with its quest for permanent certainties from Critical Historical Mindedness with its continuous quest for more comprehensive understanding.

3. I have drawn on ancient, modern, and contemporary authors for these reflections on American democracy. Among the most important are Plato, Aristotle, The Federalist Papers, Alexis de Tocqueville, Hannah Arendt, Charles Taylor, E. J. Dionne, William Galston, Jane Mayer, George Packer, Benjamin Barber, and Michael Sandel. For the negative effects of bias on human inquiry and conduct, see Lonergan's *Insight: A Study in Human Understanding*.

4. This list of cultural and institutional challenges is meant to be illustrative and not exhaustive.

5. For a persuasive critique of this anti-government ideology, see Thomas Mann and Norman Ornstein, *It's Even Worse Than It Looks*, Basic Books, 2012. And their even more critical sequel, *It's Even Worse Than It Was*.

6. Though the Biden Administration has preserved the unity of NATO and the European Union in supporting Ukraine against the Russian invasion, the long-term stability of these important alliances is far from assured.

7. While the American left are often guilty of rhetorical excess and lack of political realism, the hard right's reliance on lies and conspiracy theories is deliberately divisive.

8. Though Orban's authoritarian rule in Hungary makes him an outlier in the European Union, he's been warmly welcomed as a nationalist model by many American conservatives today.

9. The Democrats also struggle to combine strong support for traditionally excluded groups (blacks, lesbians and gays, the urban poor) with a convincing and unifying national policy agenda directed to the common good of all Americans. E. J. Dionne, in his recent *Code Red*, wisely encourages moderates and progressives to unite politically in the era of Trump. The dangers created by their political divisions are very high.

10. See Thomas Mann's and Norman Ornstein's *It's Even Worse Than It Was* and *It's Even Worse Than It Looks*, where they argue for the asymmetrical extremism between the Republican and Democratic parties since the era of Reagan. Trump's evident unfitness for the presidency, both intellectual and moral, also points to the troubling penetration of our politics by America's celebrity culture.

11. From the beginning, America has struggled to combine the Capitalist celebration of calculated "self-interest" with the Democratic emphasis on "the common good." The illusion of "market fundamentalism" is that the pursuit of self-interest leads naturally to the comprehensive and enduring public good.

12. See especially Chapter 4 in this book for Lonergan's critical distinction between "essential" and "effective" freedom.

13. The fragility of democracies and their vulnerability to demagogues and tyrants is a recurrent theme in political theory, beginning with Plato's critique of democracy in Book VIII of the *Republic*. But it received particular emphasis between the two World Wars when fledgling liberal democracies failed in Germany, Italy, and Spain. The disturbing results of the prolonged Arab Spring only highlight these enduring challenges.

14. A major theme of Charles Taylor's great work, *Sources of the Self*, is that the moral aspirations of Modernity require a sustaining moral ontology that modern skepticism and cultural suspicion tend to subvert. "High moral standards require strong moral sources." An essential part of our civic education is cultivating in the young a deepened and enduring respect for them both.

Chapter 2

The Nature and Purpose
of a Liberal Education

This seminal chapter is a revised version of a Convocation address I gave to the Vassar community in 1992.[1] After thirty years as a student and teacher of the liberal arts, I had wanted to share with my colleagues and our students my personal understanding of what we were doing together. Thus, these fundamental reflections on the nature, purpose, and singular importance of a liberal education.

In this extended revision, I have a very large audience in mind. Students presently in college or preparing to begin their higher education. Their parents and their high school teachers. The dedicated college teachers who are presently educating their peers and siblings. And the adult citizens of our democracy who need to understand the essential connection between liberal education and responsible citizenship. Because my remarks at Vassar were originally inspired by three highly personal events, I have decided to preserve part of the prologue to my convocation address in this seminal chapter.

These reflections on liberal education have their source in three quite different experiences. The first experience is rooted in friendship. Several summers ago, I decided with a few of my college friends from Notre Dame to gather at least once a year for an extended weekend, an informal unstructured reunion. In September of 1991, ten of us assembled at a summer home near Centerville on Cape Cod. The year before we met on the island of Jamaica in the Caribbean where one of my classmates, a former lawyer, then owned a seaside restaurant. The most significant moments of each reunion were the long animated conversations in which we talked late into the night about everything that really matters to us: our changing lives, our families, the demands and satisfactions of work, our faith or loss of faith, our sense, as we then approached fifty, of the contracting future. But mostly we talked of the great and common world from which we had come and to which we would soon return.[2]

Each reunion raised the same question for me. What was it about our college experience that had bound the ten of us together through time and change; that made us willing to travel great distances for the sake of each other's company; that made us eager to reenact the bonding experience of shared conversation that we had begun thirty years earlier on the plains of northern Indiana?

The second experience is rooted in parenthood, in being the father of three daughters, the eldest who had recently graduated from college and her sisters then studying in New England. During the previous eight years, my wife and I, together with our daughters, had visited over twenty-five liberal arts colleges: from Middlebury in northern Vermont to Georgetown in the nation's capital. From Swarthmore near Philadelphia to Oberlin just outside Cleveland. Our college trips tended to follow a recurrent pattern. They all began with a long and surprisingly welcome drive. Our confinement to the car together provided a rare and lovely opportunity to talk with our children without the interruptions of phone calls, the visits of friends, or the pounding rhythms of rock 'n' roll. During these long drives, an implicit question lurked constantly in the background of our talk. Why are we making this pilgrimage together? Why this extravagant expenditure of time, attention, and energy? What is it for? Why is it worth doing?[3]

The second stage of these family excursions began when we reached our destinations. The colleges themselves are singularly beautiful places, quiet and yet spirited at the same time. They are places of passage for our young people into adulthood, places through which they enter into the obligations of citizenship and the responsibilities of the common world. As many of you know, information sessions and campus tours have become a required part of the ritual. Their net effect has been to arouse perplexity in me. At one level, they are quite informative as quantitative data are in abundant supply. Numbers of applicants, average SAT scores, percentages of students admitted to professional schools, the size of the library, student/faculty ratios, a list of extracurricular activities for every conceivable student interest. As the admissions officers liked to boast, "If we don't have the particular club you want, we shall be happy to create it for you."

At the same time, the colleges are comparatively silent, almost inarticulate, about their reasons for being. As a parent and teacher, I thought that the most basic questions were rarely asked or discussed. What is the distinctive purpose of an education in the liberal arts? What is the special contribution of the liberal arts college to the formation of young adults? And is that contribution really being achieved?

The third experience has its source in my double vocation as a citizen and teacher. I had read a report, prepared by Lynne Cheney of the National Endowment for the Humanities, lamenting the cultural and historical ignorance of American college graduates. It also deplored the failure of American education to inform our students with a common fund of knowledge, a common set of arts and virtues, a common framework of discursive allusion and reference. Lynne Cheney's criticisms led me to reflect on the significance of sharing common ground and on the nature of a commonplace.[4] Trying to understand what a commonplace is, I began with my image of the Boston Common and with my memory of the commons in several small new England towns. A common seems to be a central space that belongs to all the citizens of a community, a public place shared by everyone where all can meet and gather to see and talk with each other. A place of assembly in times of joy or grief; a site that is cared for by everyone and for which all accept responsibility. In its spatial meaning then, the commonplace is the center of our shared lives as citizens, as members of a unified political body.

The word "common" is an adjective as well as a noun. In its adjectival form, it derives from the Greek term *koinon,* which is itself the linguistic root of *koinonia,* the Greek term for community.[5] The etymology is singularly appropriate, for a community is an association of diverse human beings bound together by their shared convictions and purposes. And communication is the practice of establishing enduring connections between the members of a community. True community only comes into being through attentive and respectful listening and speaking. There is no other way to achieve it, just as there is no better measure of a community's health than the quality of communication within it.[6]

The Greeks tended to measure the depth of a community by the depth of what its members shared in common. The Romans developed this insight with their insistence that memory is the faculty of human depth. Deep and enduring associations are communities of memory whose members share a common understanding and critical appreciation of their past. Unfortunately, the inverse also holds true. Communities without deeply shared memories tend to be shallow and fragile and subject to easy dissolution.

These classical insights into community have a special significance for America and American education. The United States was founded and continues to be renewed by immigrants from many different cultures. It is historically a land of strangers, coming from different places, speaking different languages, bearing different memories of the past. The enduring American challenge is clearly stated on our currency, *E pluribus unum*, out of many peoples, traditions, and languages, to create one unified national republic. Today, it is hard to resist the suspicion that the common culture defining us as Americans is primarily commercial in nature. As Americans, we no longer tend to see each other as neighbors in a town, or citizens in a republic, or children of a common God, but rather as producers and consumers gathered together in malls or stadiums, our new commonplaces, for the sharing of bread and circuses.[7]

Let me summarize the fruits of this deliberately personal prologue in a series of questions that define the thematic boundaries of this chapter. (1) What is the distinctive contribution of a college education to the formation of young adults and citizens? (2) What is the responsibility of Vassar, and other liberal arts colleges, for the creation of a common cultural inheritance? To what common memories, to what common fund of knowledge, to what common goods and responsibilities do we introduce all of our students? (3) And is there any longer a common ground within which we as adult citizens still gather, to which we invite all of our children as they come of age, and for which all of us accept personal responsibility?

There is no final answer to these perennial questions. Each generation must raise and answer them anew, as its way of keeping itself and its core traditions alive. But there are enduring insights about learning and teaching and the critical stages of human development by which any credible answer should be informed. Let me set a few of these insights before you, and then invite your thoughtful reflection upon them.[8] I'd like to explore with you six quotations, taken from very different sources and time periods, whose common thread is their connection to the liberal arts. I once thought that these statements expressed common places, uncontroversial basic truths that could be taken for granted by our fellow citizens. I am no longer confident that this is so. But I continue to believe that these truths should serve as the common ground on which every liberal arts college is founded.

The first quotation is taken from the renowned Roman orator Cicero. "We are all born male or female, but we need every art to become human." Let us start as Cicero did by focusing on the "we," the first-person plural, the appropriate language of educational thought, and a needed corrective to our vaunted American individualism. Cicero's use of the word "we" reminds us that education is always a common endeavor. It is the way a community renews itself by deliberately drawing its children into their public life.

But there is a second insight offered in the closing words of Cicero's maxim on which I want to concentrate. "We need to become human." All of us receive a biological identity at birth, but we only acquire our distinctive human identity through education and interaction with others. Education is, in fact, the communal process of forming, refining, and exercising the arts and virtues that make us genuinely human.

Cicero's insight points to an important but neglected distinction that shapes the course of human development, namely the distinction between education and learning.[9] Education is or should be a temporally limited process. It comes to an end when a human being becomes an adult and enters into the full privileges and responsibilities of the civic and cultural community. It has a distinctive purpose, to prepare us carefully for our common humanity and our shared citizenship. By contrast, learning is or should be a lifelong process. Hopefully, we will continue to study and learn for the rest of our lives. While education is a common enterprise, in learning we follow our personal interests and passions. By its nature, learning leads to specialization, to the pursuit of individual callings and to the restricted associations of professional life. If the liberal arts college is the great cultural symbol of human education, then the university graduate schools of medicine, law, engineering, business, architecture, and ministry are the symbols of specialized learning.[10]

The clear and present danger today is that our colleges will be absorbed into the professional *ethos* of the university. But the arts on which the college must concentrate, the specifically liberal arts, should be held in common, regardless of one's individual calling or profession. At too many colleges, like Vassar and others, when the most basic question about our identity is raised: What are these liberal arts? an uncomfortable silence often follows. What does this silence tell us about our power of memory, about our clarity of purpose, about our capacity to articulate our specific reasons for being?

Let us approach this elemental question of identity by recalling the answer that was traditionally given to it. According to classical sources, there are seven liberal arts divided into two groups: the arts of language, known as the *trivium,* and the arts of measurement that were called the *quadrivium.* All of the human arts are by their nature productive. In acquiring them, we learn to produce something that is well made, often something beautiful and good. The arts of language clearly allow us to do this. The art of grammar is the acquired ability to produce graceful and meaningful speech and writing, and to judge the spoken and written discourse of others. Rhetoric, the art of genuinely persuasive discourse, is the basic political art. It is an essential requirement for mature citizenship, for full and active participation in the conduct of public affairs. Logic is the art of demonstrative discourse, the acquired capacity to construct sound arguments and to judge the validity of the arguments offered by others.[11]

Among the ancient Greeks, there were four mathematical arts: arithmetic, geometry, music, and astronomy. In our time, these specific arts have become mathematical and scientific. I am referring to the arts of measurement and quantitative analysis, both algorithmic and statistical, and to the basic operations of scientific method: observation, inquiry, experimentation, discovery, the forming and confirming of explanatory hypotheses, the work of theory revision. These different arts and practices, linguistic, mathematical, and scientific, should be common to all of our graduates, whether their personal bent is toward poetry or rhetoric, or as it may be, toward biology and physics.

But why are these arts liberal? We need to know and be able to explain why they are to our students, their parents and our fellow citizens. They are liberal because their purpose is to promote and preserve effective freedom. The true aim of the liberal arts college is the effective freedom of its graduates. But what does effective freedom really mean? It means that no human being can be truly free who lacks the power cultivated by education to understand, enjoy, promote, and preserve the highest human goods. Freedom, liberality, is finally in the service of the good.[12]

But what are these highest human goods? This is a matter of intense controversy, the underlying concern of every serious human debate. My own belief, based on long experience and study, is that they surely include: enduring friendships, social justice, disinterested knowledge, an intimate and sustaining personal life, active participation in republican self-government, the enjoyment and appreciation of the creative arts, and some form of authentic faith. These goods are essential to our common humanity, and their creation, preservation, and sharing are the responsibility of us all.

Now, humility is indispensable in the practice of education. We need to acknowledge, in humility, that we are not born with the liberal arts, linguistic, mathematical, or scientific, nor are we born adept at creating and preserving the human good. We must labor with great energy to acquire the arts and virtues that humanize us by preparing us to act responsibly for the common good. Eugene O'Neill is right. "Stammering is the native eloquence of all us fog people."[13] If we are ever to transcend stammering, as individuals and as a community, we need the liberal arts that make us articulate and effectively free.

The second quotation is from Bernard Lonergan, a Canadian philosopher who died in 1984.

"Deep within us all, emergent when the noise of other appetites is stilled, there is a drive to know, to understand, to see why, to discover the reason, to find the cause, to explain. Just what is wanted has many names. In what precisely it consists is a matter of dispute. But the fact of inquiry is beyond all doubt. What better symbol could one find for this obscure, exigent, imperious drive, than a man naked, running, excitedly crying, "Eureka, I've got it?"[14]

Lonergan's quote reminds us of what should be the most passionate experience occurring at college, the periodic emergence within us of the *eros* of mind, of the intense human desire to understand. This shared intellectual desire is the source or root of disinterested inquiry. As the example of the naked Archimedes suggests, it is an ardent desire, a love of understanding for its own sake, apart from any practical use to which it may be put. Most of us will never make this desire the effective center of our lives, but it is crucial that we learn, during our years at college, how it can become the dominant passion of a single person or of a fellowship of scientists, scholars, and artists united in the pursuit of wisdom and truth.[15]

Let the *Eureka!* of Archimedes be the symbol of this cognitive passion and of the intellectual *eros* that sustains it. We can learn from the example of Archimedes several important truths:

> that human inquiry is an essentially erotic endeavor; that acts of discovery, though rarer than we desire, are often accompanied by ecstatic delight; that both inquiry and discovery promote self-transcendence, the forgetfulness of self, though the evidence for this ecstasy is generally less dramatic than Archimedes' naked dash through the streets of Syracuse. And finally, that the natural impulse of those who seek understanding is freely to share what they learn with others.[16]

In the course of our liberal education, every one of us should directly experience the *eros* of mind. It should haunt our lives and memories wherever we may go, and whatever else we may do. A liberal education should make us eager to continue the life of the mind on our own, and generously to support the numerous centers of learning in which it flourishes.

The third quotation is from the Roman statesman Cato. "Never is she more active than when she does nothing. Never is he less alone than when he is by himself."[17] Cato's paradox highlights the love of interiority, which is a mark of the liberally educated person. It also dramatizes the paradoxical nature of the act of thinking. Viewed from the outside, from the perspective of the external observer, to think is to do nothing, and to do it is to be completely alone. But lived from the inside, from the perspective of the thinker herself, she is never more active than when she is thinking and never less alone. A liberal education should prepare you for the joys of solitude, for the pleasure of your own company that is enacted in thought, when you are alone and your stereo and cell phone are finally shut off.

In one crucial respect, thinking and acting are profoundly different. Genuine thinking tends to divide the self. It awakens within us opposing voices who take different sides on the same question. It fills the mind with obstacles that require us to stop what we are doing and to think our way through them or into them. Thinking is the intense argument that I conduct with myself in the silence of solitude. Acting is unlike thinking because it tends to unite the self. It requires us to choose one road rather than another and to walk it as faithfully and as far as we can. Think of Robert Frost's poem, "The Road Not Taken." "Two roads diverged in a yellow wood, and sorry I could not travel both and be one traveler, long I stood." In thinking, I stand at the juncture where the roads diverge, and travel down each of them in imagination. But in action, I must take only one road and leave the other untraveled. Although they are structurally opposed, in the wise person thought and action seek to be friends rather than rivals. There is evidence of their friendship in a statement by Pericles now inscribed on the Leffingwell bench in the park directly across from Strong, a Vassar residence hall. "The great impediment to action, in our opinion, is not discussion but the lack of that knowledge preparatory to action which is gained by discussion: for we have the capacity to think before we act, and of acting too."[18]

The fourth quotation is from Hannah Arendt, a German Jewish émigré to the United States who died after a distinguished teaching career in 1975. "Education is the point at which we decide whether we love the world enough to assume responsibility for it, and by the same token, save it from that ruin, which, except for renewal, except for the coming of the new and the young, would be inevitable. And education, too, is where we decide whether we love our children enough not to expel them from our world and leave them to their own devices, nor to strike from their hands their chance of undertaking something new and unforeseen by us."[19]

It seems that the rhythm of adult life needs to alternate between solitude and the human circle, between time alone and time with others. This reflection of Hannah Arendt returns us from the solitude of interiority to the common ground of the world. Arendt asks us what it really means to be an educator: a parent, a teacher, a counsellor, a trusted friend.[20] Based on my experience in these interdependent roles, I believe there are common traits that should unite everyone who seeks to educate the young. A growing knowledge of the world with its complex history of greatness and wretchedness; an active love and concern for the world that emerges from this developing knowledge; a free acceptance of responsibility for the world with its constant need for reform and renewal; and finally, a love of the young who shall inherit our world and the obligation to care for it when their time comes. A very high calling all citizens share.

The fifth quotation, from the Latin author Terence, articulates an ancient insight that is beginning to be recovered in our time. "I am a human being; I find nothing human alien to me."[21]

A major task of education is to awaken within us a sympathetic understanding of the "other," an appreciation of what is different and initially alien; of cultures, countries, and regions where we are the strangers, and where we do not feel "at home." Education nearly always begins with appropriating the languages, traditions, and stories of our homeland. In this earliest phase of our development, we take possession of what our ancestors have passed on to us. We become at ease in our native land or region as we learn our way around in it. Gradually, we cease to need an external map to guide us through its geographical space, its historical time. When education is partly successful, the map exists within ourselves; we carry it with us, with all its limitations, wherever we go.[22]

In contemporary American education, this cultural appropriation process is highly partial and selective. According to Robert Bellah, the coordinating author of *Habits of the Heart*, an important study of American cultural history, there are four great traditions that have largely shaped the American character.[23] The biblical tradition of the seventeenth century Puritans; the civic republican tradition of the colonial period, which inspired the Declaration of Independence and the Federal Constitution; the commercial utilitarian tradition of the nineteenth century (Bellah cites Benjamin Franklin as its representative spokesman); and the expressive individualist tradition of Walt Whitman and the poets of the expanding frontier.

Based on considerable classroom experience, I believe that many Vassar students are largely ignorant of two of these formative traditions: the biblical tradition of early New England and the civic republican tradition of Jefferson, Adams, and Lincoln. Let me cite just one example from my own pedagogy. I regularly offered a yearly course in ethics, in which part of the curriculum was devoted to biblical morality, Hebrew and Christian. When we began to study the Bible, many of my students were suspicious of the Old and New Testaments, and unfamiliar with the symbolic resources they offer for understanding human experience. I refer to the biblical symbols of creation, sin, exile, covenant, Passover, wilderness, law, prophetic truth telling, the great commandments of love, the Christian beatitudes, the passion of Gethsemane, the law of the cross, and the resurrection. What many gradually discovered to their great surprise, and without reliance on prior religious conviction, was the power of these symbols to illuminate our lives and the state of our world. They also discovered how meagre and thin are the interpretive categories of utilitarian and expressive individualism when taken in isolation from these older American moral sources.[24]

This recurrent example makes an important point. We can be alienated and cut off not only from the history and culture of other nations, but from our own national inheritance as well. Passing over to the strange and unfamiliar, which is an essential part of education, may require passing over to repressed and neglected periods in our common history as well as to the histories and traditions of other lands. There is an unfolding rhythm of education that needs to be respected. Education begins in our homeland with the appropriation of its treasures, stories, and resources. This original appropriation, in fact, is what enables us to pass over into the wonderlands of other lives and times, of other cultures and continents, of other historical traditions and ways of life. Passing over is a complex experience, often marked by excitement, unease, and disquiet. The homeland of others is normally very different from our own. What are we to make of these discovered differences? How are we to connect our limited world with the worlds of strangers, or the neglected traditions and stories within our own country?[25]

Unless we cut the ties to our homeland, unless we become permanent residents in the various wonderlands to which we travel, the expansive process of passing over is completed by a process of critical return, of coming back. Taken together and in sequence, passing over and coming back create the conditions for "critical belonging" to the commonplace. They encourage a steady, open-eyed, realistic, and critical belonging to our native land, which is complemented by a generous understanding and appraisal of the homelands of many others.

The final quotation is from Max Weber's important work, *The Protestant Ethic and the Spirit of Capitalism.* "Specialists without spirit, sensualists without heart, this nullity imagines it has attained a level of civilization never before achieved."[26] More than a century ago, Weber warned modern Western culture of a twofold danger threatening its integrity from within. He cautioned that the marked disposition of our commercial utilitarian culture was to produce "specialists without spirit" (the technocratic and financial manager); while the parallel disposition of our expressive individualist culture was to produce "sensualists without heart" (the liberated hedonist). Let me suggest that Weber's specialists without spirit are all those cut off by the premature narrowness of their education from the common ground of the world. Those who have deprived themselves, or been deprived by their teachers, of their full educational inheritance: that includes both the arts of language and the arts of measurement, both solitude and community, both the eros of mind and commitment to action, both homeland and wonderland, both love of the young and love of the world.

And who are the "sensualists without heart"? All those who have substituted the first person singular, the "I" for the "We," in their concept of education. All who think of their education primarily as a means to self-advancement, to resume building, to personal pleasure and profit. Who emerge from their critical years in college without a devotion to the commonweal, nor a willingness to act and sacrifice for the common good. Who fail to understand that education is a common gift that we receive from our ancestors, parents, and teachers in order to transmit it enriched and enlarged to our children and their descendants.

The reason liberal education is so important, the reason we must reflect on its nature and purpose so often, the reason we quarrel about its integrity with such passion, is that it concerns the most vital human matters. The bonds of enduring friendship, both personal and civic; the developing lives of our children; the fate of our common world. When we gather at the shore with old friends, when we drive to distant colleges with our sons and daughters, and when we reflect deeply on the state of the republic, we draw on the gift of our own education, and renew our willingness to share it freely with those still unborn. Let us be faithful to this great and honorable calling. For so much is at stake, for so many people, in this critical human effort.

NOTES

1. The original Convocation address was entitled "Our Reasons For Being: Reflections on the Commonweal."

2. Enduring friendships are one of the great blessings of a liberal education. In our case, the friendships have flourished for over sixty years.

3. Educating their children well is a grave responsibility of all parents. A responsibility that yields deep and enduring rewards for the entire family.

4. Implicit in each of Cheney's criticisms was the belief that a college education should be a source of intellectual and civic community.

5. Although there are limitations to our classical Greco-Roman inheritance, there are also exceptional strengths on which we should continue, gratefully, to draw.

6. An important reason for writing this book was my growing distress at the evident decline in America's civic conversation. A decline that is discernible everywhere: in the press, social media, our political parties and institutions at all levels, and in the daily communication among our citizens. To judge by our highly divisive and partisan public discourse, American community is very weak indeed.

7. As I shall argue in chapter 7, American culture has struggled from the beginning between the economic priorities of capitalism and the very different priorities of democratic citizenship. This is a continuing struggle that clearly affects our understanding and practice of education.

8. As this book's unfolding chapters reveal, I believe that the topics they cover require both constants and variables. The constants are rooted in our common human nature; the variables in the situatedness of human persons in nature and history. By taking both dimensions seriously, I'm able to provide an account that is enduring and sensitive to change.

9. For a thoughtful account of the distinction between education and learning, see Hannah Arendt's essay, "The Crisis of Education" in her collection, *Between Past and Future*.

10. I further develop the contrast between colleges and universities in chapter 4, "Effective Freedom: What it Is and Why it Matters." For Lonergan's defense of effective freedom, see *Insight*, 623–24.

11. Several of Plato's dialogues and Aristotle's philosophical essays provide detailed accounts of these linguistic arts and of the counterfeit arts that deliberately simulate them.

12. For Bernard Lonergan's incisive account of "effective freedom," see chapter 4 of this work, and the different portions of *Insight* in which that account is developed.

13. A memorable observation of Edmond Tyrone in O'Neill's great play, *Long Day's Journey Into Night*.

14. Bernard Lonergan, *Insight*.

15. A shared respect for unrestricted inquiry and the objective knowledge to which it leads is essential to a vibrant and healthy democracy. All citizens need not be scientists, historians, or philosophers, but all should share an appreciation of what their fellow citizens do and contribute to the common world.

16. Lonergan's *Insight* is one of the best accounts that we have of the conditions, occurrence, and enduring fruits of unrestricted inquiry.

17. Hannah Arendt begins her Gifford lectures on *Thinking* with this arresting quote from Cato the Elder (234–139 BCE).

18. A statement attributed to Pericles by the Greek historian, Thucydides, in his classic *History of the Peloponnesian Wars*.

19. Hannah Arendt, "The Crisis of Education," an essay in her important collection, *Between Past and Future*.

20. Education is a process that begins at birth with our parents, is complemented by our neighbors and teachers in grade and high school, and that culminates in our intellectual and civic development in college. In all phases of our education, Arendt's three imperatives apply.

21. "Homo sum, humani nihil a me alienum puto." A quote from Terence's play, *The Self Tormentor.*

22. As important as our personal education is, it is always subject to the limitations of our culture and our teachers. For an extended development of this structural truth, see chapter 5, "The Critical Appropriation of Traditions: Reflections of a Teacher."

23. Robert Bellah et al., *Habits of the Heart*.

24. A comprehensive account of education must include the complementary realities of the individual person and the educating communities to which he/she belongs. The neglected American cultural traditions tend to be more communitarian than either Utilitarian or Expressive Individualism

25. For an insightful account of "passing over and coming back," see John Dunne's *The Way of All The Earth.*

26. Weber concludes his account of "The Iron Cage of Modernity" with this highly critical appraisal of its restricted cultural heritage.

Chapter 3

Demystifying the L-Word

The Merits and Limitations of Modern Liberalism

What do we mean when we speak of a person, a policy, a society, a mentality, or outlook, as "liberal"? I don't think there is a clear or simple answer to this question. If we look for guidance to the linguistic roots of "liberal," we find them in classical Latin, where *liber* and *liberalis* referred to a free person, that is a recognized citizen of Rome. In this respect, as in many others, the Romans were following the example of the ancient Greeks, who also reserved the title of a "free man" for a citizen, in contrast to a slave or manual laborer who lacked the common rights of citizenship. As Hegel succinctly stated: in ancient despotisms, like Persia, only one was free (the reigning despot); in the classical republics, like Athens and Rome, only a few, the male citizens, were free; but in modern republics since the American and French Revolutions the shared aspiration is that all will be free, enjoying the equal liberties, protections, and obligations of full citizens. An aspiration, as Hegel knew well, that neither then, nor now, has ever been fully realized.[1]

The restricted scope of "liberal" later reappears in the context of the Medieval University, where the "liberal arts" and "liberal studies" are reserved for those who aspire to be free: free from ignorance, parochial concerns, the narrow utilitarian outlook of trade and commerce, in order to be free for the disinterested pleasures of the mind found in liberal education and the pursuit of knowledge.[2]

While there are important contrasts between the classical and medieval perspectives, they share the common assumption that free lives, free activities, free courses of study, and free perspectives on life are reserved for the few. A central difference in the ongoing quarrel between "the ancients and the moderns" is that we moderns, for the most part, no longer accept this shared assumption. And, as a result, the semantic range of "liberal" becomes greatly extended in the modern era. The focus of this chapter will be on the internal tensions that challenge and complicate this important historical extension.

The moral and political narrative of modernity is inseparable from the history of liberalism, the dominant, though not uncontested, ethical tradition of the modern age. Although liberals are often accused of lacking a sense of history, it is impossible to understand the complexity of the liberal tradition without tracking its evolution over several centuries and within several countries. Liberalism had its origin in the seventeenth century and achieved its greatest victories over the next two hundred and fifty years. Its causal role in the tumultuous upheavals of the twentieth century remains, as we shall see, a matter of intense dispute.

There are distinct liberal traditions in Great Britain, France, Germany, and the United States. The theoretical foundations of British liberalism were laid by John Locke, Adam Smith, Jeremy Bentham, and John Stuart Mill. In France, where liberalism was never as powerful as in the British Isles, the liberal tradition appeals to the principles and arguments of Montesquieu, Constant, and Tocqueville. German liberalism was inspired by the expressivism of Von Humboldt and Herder, and the important Kantian concept of moral autonomy. As Robert Bellah has argued in *Habits of the Heart*, there are four quite different sources of American liberalism: biblical, civic republican, utilitarian, and expressive. Within different countries and at different historical periods, the aspirations and fears that galvanized liberals have varied greatly. These differences are an essential part of the liberal tradition's richness and vitality, so that, despite its internal limitations, liberalism remains an indispensable contributor to any viable democratic politics today.[3]

The history of liberalism is a study in opposition and critique. In the seventeenth century, English liberals opposed religious intolerance and monarchical absolutism. In the eighteenth century, French liberals opposed the power and privileges of the nobility and the Church. Nineteenth-century liberals throughout the West opposed the political and social dominance of the bourgeoisie and the potential despotism of democratically elected legislative majorities. Twentieth-century liberals have had a broad range of critical opponents: economic monopolies, fascist and totalitarian governments, inherited constraints on personal development and free expression, national and regional oppressors of human rights.

The core principle uniting the varieties of liberalism is a specific understanding of human liberty. Modern liberals believe that they are historical agents of liberation, freeing themselves and others from inherited forms of human domination. In this sense, liberalism is a reactive stance, more clearly defined by what it is against than what it is for. What liberals have consistently opposed is the reliance on institutional authority as a principle of public and private order. Liberals actively distrust authority; they tend to identify its exercise with paternalism, coercion, unwanted and unneeded interference, despotic control, the repression of individual action, conscience, thought, and feeling. Over time, the liberal critique of authority has shifted its principal targets, as Church, State, even the basic disciplines of civilization itself were successively identified as the enemies of individual liberty.

What are liberals historically for? Religious liberty, freedom of conscience, worship, and belief; intellectual liberty, freedom of inquiry, and public expression; political liberty, the lawful guarantee of individual rights; economic liberty, free enterprise and unregulated financial and commercial exchange; moral liberty, the freedom to shape personal life and conduct as the autonomous individual desires; geographic and social liberty, the freedom to travel and live where one pleases, and to rise above the constraining limits of an individual's racial, class, gender, or social origin.

In the broadest terms, liberals are against authority as a constraint on individual freedom, and against hierarchy as a violation of human equality. They commonly view traditional hierarchies as illegitimate, and inherited forms of authority as sources of unwarranted coercion. For liberals, the positive essence of freedom is individual autonomy. Autonomous individual choice, unrestrained by external authority in its many forms, is the substantive core of human liberty. With their free choices, individual persons define their religious, intellectual, and moral identities; they determine who they are, how, where, and with whom they will live, what they believe and value, how they spend their money and time. Thus, the more individuals govern themselves and the less they are governed by the power of others, the freer they become.[4]

Several factors account for the liberal critique of authority and hierarchy. Liberalism is primarily, though not exclusively, a child of the European Enlightenment. It shares the early modern distrust of what Hannah Arendt calls the Roman Trinity, religion, tradition, and authority, the principal sources of communal cohesion and continuity in medieval Europe.[5] Liberals also share the cognitive skepticism of the empiricist tradition. They openly challenge the legitimating arguments for nearly all forms of public authority. Their epistemic distrust extends to the Church's reliance on sacred scripture and divine revelation, the state's reliance on prudent and impartial economic planning, the social majority's reliance on inherited laws and customs.

The earliest forms of European liberalism also relied on what Charles Taylor calls "the punctual conception of the self."[6] On this conception, rooted in Descartes and Locke, the disembodied and socially disengaged ego, the punctual self, is asserted to be the exclusive bearer of human value and meaning. Since nature, as conceived by Newton and early modern physics, and the conflicting plurality of inherited cultural traditions were explicitly rejected as reliable sources of moral knowledge, right and wrong, good and evil, just and unjust were now to be determined solely by the autonomous choices of the isolated subject. In English liberalism, the punctual self, the solitary individual, was construed as the bearer of natural rights, including the right to life, liberty, and property.[7] The only recognized purpose of government was to guarantee these individual rights and keep them secure. By contrast, there were no natural or intrinsic obligations binding on the punctual self. All legitimate human obligations were said to have their origin in the individual's tacit or explicit consent to enforceable rules. This influential conception, of original or "natural" rights without corresponding moral and political obligations, helps to explain the liberal reliance on social contract theories, in which isolated individuals supposedly establish political communities for their mutual protection against death, violence, theft, and unwarranted interference with their freedom of choice.[8]

Throughout Europe and North America, the earliest disciples of liberalism were drawn from the middle class. In England, middle-class Puritans revolted against Roman and Anglo Catholic Catholicism, and the Anglo Catholic support for the prerogatives of monarchy. The French bourgeoisie were equally opposed to the inherited privileges and power of nobles, clerics, and kings. In the United States, the struggle for independence from Great Britain was led by New England colonists like John Adams who bridled at the crown's interference in colonial affairs. The deeply influential Kantian principle of moral autonomy is also no respecter of inherited title or office. Kant held that every human being is morally independent, capable of determining the substance and spirit of the moral law through the exercise of pure practical reason alone. Thus, by quite different paths, the Protestant opposition to Catholic hierarchies, the democratic opposition to monarchical government, and the Kantian opposition to heteronomous moral sources effectively converged to shape the expanding liberal alliance.

The rise of liberalism also coincided with an unprecedented concern for the individual self. The Protestant Reformation insisted on the inviolability of individual conscience; Enlightenment critics insisted on the independence of individual inquiry: capitalists insisted on the individual's freedom of economic behavior and choice: the champions of democracy insisted on the lawful guarantee of individual rights: Kant insisted on the moral liberty of the autonomous rational will. For the liberal tradition, there is no higher value than the discrete autonomous individual, the bearer of inalienable rights, and the subject of self-determining choice.

The liberal hostility to government has additional roots in the history of European capitalism. In Locke's *Second Treatise on Government*, the legitimate powers of the state are limited to protecting the natural rights of its citizens, particularly the right to private property. In Adam Smith's *The Wealth of Nations*, governments are admonished not to interfere with the voluntary transactions of the market place. The classical liberalism of the eighteenth century treats the commercial exchange market as the central institution of a free society. Invoking the principle of *laissez-faire,* classical liberals rely on the rational choices of self-interested individuals to satisfy private desires and to maximize national wealth. For them, it is the "invisible hand" of the unregulated market, rather than the intrusive hand of government, that promotes the enduring public goods of prosperity and wealth.

The presumed benevolence of capitalism and the sacredness of private property came under critical scrutiny during the Industrial Revolution of the nineteenth century. Although proponents of *laissez-faire* remained the dominant political force, the liberal tradition became more socially and historically minded, and more open to political reform. Nineteenth-century liberals, like John Stuart Mill, appealed to the principle of utility, the greatest happiness of the greatest number, in judging the merits of competing economic and political arrangements. To check the power of economic monopolies that distort the working of the market, progressive liberals in the United States campaigned for anti-trust laws and increased government regulation of land, commerce, and industry. During the Great Depression of the 1930s, Franklin Roosevelt's New Deal deliberately experimented with a mixed economy to remedy the abuses and inequities of unregulated capitalism. These public responses to economic insecurity and glaring social injustice gradually led to the creation of moderate welfare states in Europe and North America, and to an historic and persisting division within the liberal tradition. This division pits classical economic liberals, committed to minimal government and *laissez-faire,* against social justice or welfare liberals who support progressive taxation and a reliable public safety net largely administered by officers of the state.

This contentious and unresolved division in political philosophy and economic policy is actually an intramural debate. Today's "economic conservatives" and libertarians are really classical liberals who reject the welfare state and the expansion of government power it requires. Contemporary "economic liberals," or "progressives" in the idiom of the moment, are often defenders of a mixed economy who accept free enterprise, but oppose the glaring inequities of capitalism in both the national and global economy. While social justice liberals want to balance the advantages of free enterprise with the political and social requirements of democratic equity, classical liberals argue that a free society works best under minimal government and maximal liberty of individual choice.[9]

Twentieth-century liberalism has had a complex and evolving relation with the challenges of pluralism. As the century advanced, the oppositional focus of liberals successively shifted from resistance to corporate and financial monopolies during the Great Depression, to a spirited defense of liberal democracy in response to Hitler, Mussolini, and Stalin, then to the global anti-colonial movement after World War II, finally, to the daunting demands of moral and cultural pluralism by the century's end.

In the second half of the nineteenth century, powerful economic monopolies were created in Europe and North America. These trusts, as they were called, clearly violated the principles of free market competition on which Adam Smith had insisted. Monopolies effectively dominated the market, controlling prices, wages, and profits, amassing scandalous wealth and irresistible political influence. The original "progressive" movement within the liberal tradition formed in opposition to these trusts that exercised despotic control over the nation's economic and political activity. To check and reverse the monopoly power of the trusts, the progressives argued for greater taxing authority as well as greater government oversight and regulation. They rejected *laissez-faire*, the normative basis of classical liberalism, as a dogmatic principle that had outlived its utility. To replace it, they began to advocate for the constitutive elements of a mixed or pluralistic economy: free enterprise in the context of fair competition, active governmental scrutiny and regulative authority over commerce and industry, progressive federal taxation, independent labor unions to bargain for workers' wages and working conditions. Despite intense corporate and financial opposition, Montesquieu's political principle of institutional checks and balances was gradually introduced into national economic practice. As the original progressive movement gained greater public support, its policy objectives shifted from restraining monopoly power to creating the basic security protections of the moderate welfare state.[10]

The most threatening challenge to liberal democracy emerged in the 1930s. World War I had decimated the territory and populations of the great powers. The peace treaty that concluded the war proved to be punitive and unworkable. In Germany and Italy, national unrest was compounded by severe inflation, economic depression, and extreme unemployment. Parliamentary democracies throughout Europe seemed impotent in the face of the social and economic crises demoralizing their people. As public confidence in democratic institutions declined, radical political "solutions" gained favor. The Bolshevik Revolution in Russia was followed by the political successes of Mussolini, Hitler, and Franco. For many frightened Europeans, it seemed that only ruthless despotic governments and leaders were equal to meeting the deepening economic and political challenges of that perilous time.

Internally divided along class and ideological lines and paralyzed by memories of the Great War, the Western democracies were initially ineffective in opposing the new dictatorships. It finally required the uneasy alliance of Great Britain, the United States, and the Soviet Union to defeat Nazism, fascism, and Japanese militarism. At World War II's end, as the horrors of the "final solution" and the Stalinist terror became publicly known, the core liberal principles, widely abandoned between the world wars, were strongly reaffirmed. These principles, originally articulated to check monarchical despotism in England and France, were now seen as the necessary bulwark against the totalitarian menace. The post-war liberal consensus, the unifying basis of the North Atlantic Alliance, actively supported the basic elements of political pluralism: limited constitutional government, secure individual rights, an independent judiciary and civil society, the broad distribution of public power and the broadly shared benefits it creates, economic, political, and cultural.

The military defeat of the Axis powers had another unexpected consequence. The liberal principles invoked by the allies in their struggle against Hitler, Mussolini, and Tojo were clearly inconsistent with European colonial practice in Asia and Africa. This historic inconsistency became politically relevant when anti-colonial independence movements gained popular support in Indo-China, the Indian subcontinent and much of Africa and Asia. In the three decades after the war, the British, the French, the Dutch, the Belgians, and finally the Portuguese reluctantly accepted the loss of their overseas empires, as a plethora of post colonial states transformed the political landscape of the earth. Western liberals were internally divided by these important events. Because the independence movements in the "Third World" were actively supported by the Soviet Union and often justified in Marxist or Socialist categories, liberal adherence to the principle of national self-determination was often compromised by fear of communism or communist influence. Thus, the anti-colonial thrust of liberalism was frequently checked by its anti-Communist suspicions and anxieties. This troubling liberal dilemma reached its tragic climax with the American engagement in Vietnam, a traumatic military and political defeat that contributed to dissolving the political consensus within the United States that had emerged with the New Deal.

That consensus was also threatened by the challenges of religious and cultural pluralism. The original Western liberals were mostly Protestant Christians. Adherents of the "reform" tradition first called for religious toleration, embraced the discoveries of the new physics, supported the market economy, challenged the prerogatives of monarchy, and distanced themselves from cultural and institutional hierarchies across the board. Protestants were at ease, as Catholics often were not, with the new individualism, whether utilitarian or expressive in nature. They defended individual liberties and rights, including the right to autonomy of conscience in matters of faith and morals.

But the Christian grip on the liberal imagination weakened dramatically during the last two centuries. Several factors help to explain the erosion of this earlier alliance: the growing secularization of the European public realm, the steady expansion of the bourgeois ethic of self-interest, the apparent conflict between modern science and traditional religious beliefs, and between biblical narratives and critical historiography, the radical critique of Christianity by Marx, Nietzsche, and Freud, the religious alienation of the European working class, the basic tension between liberal moral and historical optimism and the Christian emphasis on finitude and sin. While many liberals remained genuine Christians, the historic bond between the two communities had severely frayed.

The growing estrangement between liberalism and orthodox Christianity contributed to an unprecedented moral pluralism. In the 1830s, Alexis de Tocqueville had argued that despite their political differences the people of North America were profoundly united by their common religious and moral convictions. One hundred and ninety years later that unified religious and moral community no longer exists. It has been steadily eroded by mounting intellectual skepticism, a pervasive cultural relativism, sweeping demographic changes in the composition of the American populace, and by the liberal embrace of moral autonomy as a regulative ideal.

The most prominent and persuasive advocate for contemporary moral pluralism is Isaiah Berlin, a Russian Jewish émigré to Great Britain.[11] Berlin was a liberal in the Mill tradition, a staunch opponent of totalitarianism and an equally staunch advocate of "negative liberty," the right of individuals to be left alone in a private sphere of independent reflection and choice. Berlin was not a moral skeptic. He believed in the objective reality of good and evil, right and wrong. But he was a moral pluralist who insisted on an irreducible diversity of human goods and ways of life. In contrast to classical pluralists, like Aristotle, Berlin did not believe in an objective hierarchy among these goods, nor in an integrated moral order where each good had its proper and limited place. He emphasized the tragic dimension of moral life; genuine goods are often mutually exclusive, and moral agents have to choose among them without the directive guidance of objective moral criteria.

In this brief historical survey, we have emphasized the internal complexity and numerous tensions within the liberal tradition. We have shown, I think, that there is no clear and simple answer to the basic question: what do liberals stand for? Western liberals should be distinguished from one another by geographical setting and historical period, and by their specific adherence to opposing conceptions of the person and the political community. The history of liberalism is as nuanced as the history of modernity to which it is inseparably tied, for the varieties of liberalism rely on distinctively modern conceptions of the self, society, economics, morality, and government. Liberals tend to share the modern distrust of religion, tradition, and authority, as well as the modern confidence in individual autonomy and self-determining choice. They also share the modern belief in progress, scientific, technological, and economic, the proud conviction that human existence is materially improving and that human liberties are steadily expanding and becoming more secure. Despite the unprecedented terrors of the twentieth century and the unresolved intramural debates among its contemporary adherents, liberalism, in its diverse and evolving forms, remains the dominant moral and political tradition of the modern age.

A DISORIENTING BLEND OF GREATNESS AND WRETCHEDNESS: MODERN LIBERAL SOCIETIES AND THE LIBERAL TRADITION

Although liberalism, in its diverse expressions, is clearly the most influential political tradition in modernity, it is not without its critical detractors. Pointed criticism extends not only to liberal societies, but also to the legitimating principles that provide their reasons for being. For civic humanists, like Hannah Arendt, liberal theories typically subordinate politics to economics, while liberal societies measure their communal health by reductive economic criteria.[12] But civic humanists are only one group of liberalism's critics. Communitarians, like Robert Bellah, criticize liberal individualism in both its utilitarian and expressive embodiments.[13] Marxists claim that the liberal focus on legal and political equality consistently obscures or minimizes the dehumanizing consequences of capitalism's economic inequities. Disciples of Nietzsche scorn the liberal emphasis on material comfort, the pitiable moral outlook of the "last man." Cultural conservatives challenge the rootlessness and permissiveness of liberal societies, their reflexive resistance to stabilizing moral and religious authority. Orthodox Jews, evangelical Christians, and devout Muslims reject liberal societies for their materialism, consumerism, and secularism. And historically minded Aristotelians, like Alasdair MacIntyre, highlight the incoherence of liberal moral and political theories, whether they are based on the problematic concept of "utility" or the fiction of "natural" (pre-social) rights.[14]

Even thoughtful defenders of liberalism are disquieted by the cultural and institutional pathologies that threaten the democratic West: pervasive crime and mass incarceration, the regular abuse of alcohol and narcotics, the systemic erosion of marriage and the family, the rising cost and intellectual decline of public education, the scandal of modern electoral politics, mounting public and private debt, the sensationalism and vulgarity of the communications media, the demand overload on the institutions and resources of government, the threatening ecological effects of unregulated economic activity with the dangerous global warming it continues to cause, the frequent abuse of authority by public officials, corporate and financial executives, as well as religious and cultural leaders, the barbarism and incivility of popular entertainment, the deliberately divisive uses and effects of social media.

There is considerable merit to these intellectual and cultural criticisms. As Charles Taylor has argued, the discord, fragmentation, and instability of modern liberal societies reflect the tangled legacy of modernity itself. In Taylor's judgment, the modern world has replaced the classical conception of the human good, most fully articulated in Greek philosophy and medieval theology, with a hybrid notion largely dependent on enlightenment and romantic principles. "Liberalism," in the broadest sense, is an umbrella term for the dominant modern conception of how to live now. It is a complex moral tradition in its own right that deeply informs the public and private lives of democratic citizens today.[15]

For Taylor, neither the "boosters" of modernity, like the technological gurus and cognitive and moral relativists (one thinks of Max Weber's haunting description of "specialists without spirit and sensualists without heart"), nor the unsparing critics of modernity, really understand the inherent strengths and dangers of modern liberal societies. In their different ways, they both oversimplify; the boosters by denying the serious dilemmas modern societies face, the critics, by denying the validity of the goods those societies embody. Taylor's philosophical project, a project I strongly endorse, is to develop a discriminating and critical portrait of the modern moral identity. In this portrait, both the merits and limitations of liberal democracies are clearly acknowledged. In a sense, Taylor is offering late Western modernity what Tocqueville offered early American democracy: unsparing but sympathetic criticism. " Men will not receive the truth from their enemies. And it is very rarely offered to them by their friends."[16]

Perhaps, the best way to understand modern liberal democracies is to articulate their moral aspirations, the range of human goods to which they are culturally and institutionally committed. Let us briefly examine four of these important goods: democratic self-government, government of, by, and for the people; individual liberty, the responsible, self-accountable exercise of personal freedom; material security and prosperity, affirming the basic goods of ordinary life for all citizens; a broad range of relatively autonomous human practices, scientific, cultural, charitable, political and spiritual, with each collaborative domain having its distinctive aims and internal norms of appraisal.

Each type of good is embodied in and supported by the characteristic institutions of liberal society: (a) a limited, constitutional, representative government based on multi-party democracy and nearly universal suffrage; (b) a constitutionally supported legal order that protects individual rights, with an independent judiciary to check the dangers of legislative and executive despotism; (c) a free enterprise economy with a global market in goods and services subject to governmental regulation and oversight; the market economy is importantly augmented by a complex social safety net based on the collaboration of governmental and non-governmental institutions; and (d) a dynamic and independent civil society that mediates the complex transitions between individual citizens, voluntary associations and their respective governments.[17]

The vigilant scrutiny of liberal societies is essential because of their inherent tendency to excess. Each of the human goods we have identified is subject to distortion and imbalance. There is, therefore, an enduring need for *ethical articulation* to distinguish clearly the legitimate from the illegitimate forms of these competing goods. But Taylor repeatedly insists that the aberrant or excessive forms of these modern goods do not undermine the validity of these goods in their authentic embodiment. To take one example that Taylor subtly explores: in appraising Nietzsche's influential critique of the Christian virtues, it is critical to distinguish what Nietzsche calls *ressentiment* from genuine Christian compassion modeled on the *agape* of Jesus' public ministry.

What are the notable examples of moral and political distortion in modern liberal democracies? (1) Responsible freedom easily lapses into narcissistic individualism, the confusion of personal license with authentic ordered liberty; (2) Constitutional government often declines into a remote, impersonal bureaucratic state heavily influenced by corporate wealth, professional lobbyists, and organized interest groups; (3) Free market economies regularly produce unjust patterns of distribution and reward; they are repeatedly tempted by economic imperialism, the hegemony of the market mentality, in which all human transactions are modeled on commercial exchange and everything is treated as a commodity for sale; (4) Necessary provisions for public welfare and social assistance to families and children can unintentionally create a culture of multi-generational dependency; (5) The voluntary associations that constitute a thriving civil society can deteriorate into sectarian pressure groups imposing their limited and narrow aims on public policy; and (6) Persistent racial, gender, and ethnic prejudices can promote an internally divided democracy, incapable of reaching consensus on critical matters of public policy and practice.[18]

Both the pluralism of modern societies and their evident susceptibility to excess and distortion demonstrate the vital importance of liberal and civic education. To respond critically to modern goods in both their genuine and aberrant forms, democratic citizens need a complex set of personal and public virtues. Far more than just the hallowed virtues of bourgeois liberalism (tolerance, honesty, thrift, moderation, respect for individual conscience) are required. A discriminating democratic pluralism also requires *phronesis*, the critical virtue of practical wisdom, and the cardinal virtues, courage, self-control, justice, liberality of spirit, that are needed to foster and sustain it.

Responsible democratic citizens need to cultivate their powers of independent reflection and judgment; they must learn to balance the need for personal commitment and allegiance with an openness to critical inquiry and political dissent. The health and integrity of important liberal institutions, like the market economy and the democratic state, greatly depend on the exercise of public virtues, such as critical patriotism, a strong commitment to economic and political justice, a fiduciary concern for the enduring needs of posterity, what Robert Bellah and Erik Erikson have called a citizenship of comprehensive care and public service.[19]

Now, it must be emphasized that we are not born with any of these indispensable virtues or commitments. They need to be deliberately fostered if they are to become a reliable part of each citizen's personal and civic character. This salient fact highlights the great importance of intellectual, moral, and political formation in democratic societies. The formative associations in liberal democracies need to be schools of civic virtue where democratic citizens and democratic communities learn to be intellectually, morally, and politically sound, and responsibly free.[20]

Concretely, this requires strong and cohesive families, spiritually vital religious communities, meaningful and challenging places of work, local deliberative assemblies (what Tocqueville called the "grammar schools of liberty"), colleges and universities that deliberately educate their students to know, love, and serve the world, a free and responsible press that informs, refines, and enlarges public opinion and judgment rather than emphasizing conflicts, maximizing profits, or pandering to the transient tastes and prejudices of a mass audience.

The cultural associations of a liberal democracy not only form human character, for good or ill, but they also demand exceptional virtues from their own members. To take one example, parents cannot raise intellectually sound and morally responsible children without exercising themselves the virtues of fidelity, practical wisdom, self-restraint, and non-possessive love. Thus, liberal democracies are faced with an inescapable dilemma. They need strong and independent civil societies where the relevant virtues are practiced and effectively transmitted across the generations, while the conduct of their leading public institutions makes the exercise of these demanding virtues difficult or often impossible. This danger is particularly acute when their core institutions deteriorate into their aberrant forms, for neither a remote, impersonal, interest-driven government, nor a profit-driven market economy, nor a culture of individual narcissism and moral license has any hope of creating the virtues and sustaining the allegiances that a sound and just democracy requires.[21]

This structural democratic dilemma is compounded by the endemic weaknesses of liberal theory, what Taylor describes as the "political ontology" of liberalism. Liberal theorists tend to ignore or explicitly subvert the basic requirements of a responsible democracy. To be specific: (1) Contemporary procedural liberalism tends to identify virtue-based public philosophies with repressive moral orthodoxy; (2) Procedural liberalism, in turn, relies on morally neutral procedural rules to resolve important public conflicts, and neglects the deliberate formation of responsible adults and citizens; (3) Liberal theorists seek to anchor their theoretical and practical arguments in highly dubious categories and principles, e.g., utility, the state of nature, natural rights, the social contract, enlightened self-interest, *laissez-faire*; (4) They also confuse the legitimate separation of church and state with the privatizing of religion, and frequently seek to exclude important religious perspectives and concerns from the struggles of public life; and (5) They also tend to conflate the public realm in a democratic society with the conduct of state or government, thereby neglecting the important political contributions of voluntary associations and the intermediary powers of civil society.[22]

Despite these significant weaknesses in liberal theory and practice, I want to acknowledge, together with Taylor, the historical achievements of Western liberalism. These achievements constitute part of the enduring greatness of liberal democracies, and they stand as a rebuke to any one-sided or wholesale rejection of the modern liberal tradition.

1. Liberalism has historically defended religious toleration and freedom of worship and conscience.
2. It forcefully defended intellectual liberty, unrestricted freedom of inquiry and expression, as essential conditions of personal and public development.
3. It helped to establish limited constitutional governments founded on the core principles of subsidiarity and the separation of powers. On balance, liberals have been sensitive to the dangers of concentrated political power, but much less wary of economic monopolies and trusts and their inordinate and controlling influence on democratic governments.
4. In principle, it insisted on the rule of law (not men) and the equal treatment of all citizens under the law.
5. It developed and articulated a bill of individual rights or legally secured civil and political liberties.
6. It effectively opposed the arbitrary reduction of personal choices and socio-economic opportunities due to race, gender, religion, and economic origin.
7. It affirmed the ethical importance of "ordinary life," of companionate marriage and the family, of productive and justly remunerated work, and of a broad range of social and cultural activities.
8. It encouraged the ideal of responsible personal freedom, but regularly neglected the intellectual, moral, and civic education that underlies and sustains authentic liberty. In its opposition to despotic authority and repressive orthodoxy, liberalism has often unwisely rejected the validity of authority and hierarchy as such.

9. While embracing and encouraging the free expression of critical dissent, liberals frequently lapse into an adversarial suspicion towards all forms of government and public authority.

The great strength of liberalism has been its opposition to arbitrary and despotic power, and its support for secure individual liberty. Its historic weakness has been its intellectual dependence on a reductive anthropology and sociology, the atomized conception of the unsituated punctual self, and an uncritical and limited theory of human freedom. These dependencies have made it difficult for liberal societies to achieve an enduring and essential ethical balance: that combines freedom with responsibility, liberty with justice, and individual rights with strong political and social obligations.

Contemporary liberal theory needs a strong infusion of communitarian and civic republican insights. It needs to recognize the depth of human inter-dependence and the critical role of civic, moral, and religious virtues in achieving effective freedom. It needs to develop a much richer understanding of the public realm and of the important human goods that depend for their existence on sustained public cooperation. Finally, it needs a more exigent conception of democratic citizenship and a renewed commitment to the centrality of the common good in the context of a deeply unsettled global society.

In short, liberals need to acknowledge the reciprocal connection between authentic personal development and vibrant and inclusive democratic communities at every level of human belonging and engagement. To remedy the dangerous and enduring discontents of liberal democracy will require a sustained and collaborative civic effort, with a special emphasis on promoting "liberal education at the level and demands of our time."

NOTES

1. An important argument of my book is that all three elements in this triad are equally important in a sound democracy: individual rights, secure legal and political protections, and broadly accepted personal responsibilities.

2. The relevant contrast here is between necessary, useful, and liberal.

3. My own defense of liberal democracy requires the careful integration of both the liberal and civic republican traditions. See chapter 7 in particular.

4. I find persuasive, given the realities of human development and education, Hannah Arendt's argument that a credible account of human freedom must combine both effective authority and personal liberty.

5. See Hannah Arendt, *Between Past and Future*, for a fuller account of the Roman Trinity.

6. See Charles Taylor, *Sources of the Self.*

7. John Locke is the central figure in this important stage of liberal political theory. See John Locke's *Second Treatise on Government*.

8. The background assumptions of modern social contract theories are made explicit in chapter 8, "Our Search for Wisdom: The Stories We Live By."

9. In the context of American history, the struggle has been to combine limited government with liberty and justice for all our citizens. In the protracted era of Ronald Reagan's influence, the Republican party has often narrowly defined liberty as "freedom from the federal government's authority."

10. This was clearly the principal objective behind Lyndon Johnson's Great Society initiatives.

11. See Isaiah Berlin's "Two Concepts of Liberty."

12. See chapter 7, "The Cultural Struggle for American Democracy."

13. See "The Common Good: An Exercise in Critical Retrieval" in Michael McCarthy's *Toward a Catholic Christianity*.

14. See Alasdair Macintyre's *After Virtue*.

15. Taylor articulates this critical analysis in several works but most forcefully in *Sources of the Self*.

16. Alexis de Tocqueville, *Democracy in America*.

17. See Taylor's *Sources of the Self and The Ethics of Authenticity*.

18. For these and other forms of democratic failure, see the Introduction to this book.

19. See Robert Bellah's *Habits of the Heart* and Erik Erikson's emphasis on the importance of "generativity" in human development.

20. Nearly all of this vital educational formation is neglected by traditional social contract theories.

21. Though my emphasis in this work is on the specific contribution of liberal education to responsible democratic citizenship, these important agents of civil society also play an essential role.

22. For Taylor's important distinction between ontology and advocacy, see Charles Taylor's "Cross Purposes: The Liberal-Communitarian Debate."

Chapter 4

Effective Freedom

What it Is and Why it Matters

"It is concern for the future that drives our thought back into the past, even to the remotest antiquity."

Alexis de Tocqueville, *Democracy in America*, Vol II, 349.

LIBERAL EDUCATION

What is always at stake in a discussion of liberal education is our understanding of the human person and of the concrete conditions required for human development and well-being.[1] When our concept of the human subject and our grasp of human freedom narrows, our educational practice invariably contracts. Such a contraction has, I believe, occurred in our time, with a subsequent reduction in our appreciation of the liberal arts, and of the colleges that still bear their name. Conversely, a shared commitment to the full dignity of human beings and the greatness of their calling elevates our vision of the liberal arts colleges within which they intellectually and morally mature. Our passionate debates about the nature and purpose of higher education are finally rooted in opposing philosophical accounts of the human person and the full requirements of authentic freedom. In this important chapter, deeply informed by Bernard Lonergan's enduring insights, I want to explore and articulate these critical inter-connections.[2]

It is necessary, first, to locate the liberal arts college within the broader framework of human development to which it belongs. In Western culture, the deliberate attempt to form intellectual and moral character, to cultivate the arts and virtues required for a free and full human life, is called education.

59

And there are many communal sources of education on which we regularly rely: families, neighborhoods, social and civic communities, churches, mosques, synagogues, and, of course, schools. It is worth repeating the essential truth that schools are but one of the means of education. Being one of many, however, does not lessen their importance. In the matrix of education, schools stand between the private realm of the family and the public world of politics, culture, religion, economics, and specialized research. At their different levels, schools exist to prepare young people for the opportunities and obligations of the public world. The teachers in our schools should be representatives of that world who know what the world contains, how it has evolved, what its treasures and perils are, and the arts and virtues one needs to navigate effectively within it. Education, as opposed to human learning, comes to an end when our teachers cease to be the representatives of a common body of knowledge and virtues for which every adult citizen is responsible. Learning, of course, should continue as long as human beings are alive, but education should end when the young person has intellectually and politically come of age.[3]

At its best, the liberal arts college should be the climax of education. The college's primary function is to ensure that its graduates are our intellectual, moral, and political peers, that they are prepared for the responsibilities and privileges of citizenship and can be trusted as custodians of the world's treasures and history. Viewed from this political and cultural perspective, the college has a grave obligation to the world that it claims to satisfy at its annual commencement. At commencement, the college gives a solemn assurance to those who morally and financially sustain it. "We have met our obligations to you and to our students. Our graduates have the knowledge, skills, and habits of mind and heart that are required for their complex political vocation. They also have developed the powers of discernment and judgment required for their personal and public lives. They have appropriated the common cultural heritage needed for active membership in a civilized community. If they meet their obligations to succeeding generations, the intellectual, civic and cultural fellowship we share with them will continue to thrive." What should commence when education ends are the lives of reliable, independent, and critical young adults equipped to meet their responsibilities as public and private persons.

It is no longer common practice to consider liberal education within any larger worldly framework than the economic. To judge by contemporary discourse, college students today seem chiefly to be preparing for the world of work.[4] Given the uncertain state of our economy, the costs of higher education, and the heavy debt both students and their parents assume, this narrow emphasis is understandable. Yet, it represents a severe contraction in our understanding of our students and the proper purposes of college. My emphasis, by contrast, is on the student as a free and responsible intellectual, moral, and political agent. Students, of course, have to earn a living when they graduate from college, and many have to earn it while they are studying in college, but the college's primary purpose is not economic.[5] While respecting and addressing legitimate economic realities and demands, colleges should calmly tell their students, their parents, and their future employers that vocational training is not their central concern. In the fevered cultural climate created by global capitalism, economic insecurity, and the new information technology, we risk forgetting this seminal principle. But the critical point is basic. Our different cultural institutions have different cultural functions. Each institution should concentrate on its primary cultural purpose. As churches exist to draw human beings closer to God and their neighbors, and families exist to support the intimacy of couples, the nurture of children and the protection of the elderly, so liberal arts colleges exist to complete the intellectual, political, and cultural apprenticeship of their students.[6]

Economic and vocational pressures are not the only threats that liberal arts colleges must resist. A more subtle challenge to their true identity comes from within their own ranks. College faculties are often tempted to confuse their educational mission with that of the university.[7] A liberal arts college is not a mini-university. In the province of higher learning, colleges and universities have importantly different functions. Universities are properly organized to promote the advancement of knowledge. They operate by the division of labor, dividing their members into specialized disciplines, because that has proven to be the best design for cognitive collaboration and progress. They are centers for specialized scholars and scientists, where experts pursue advanced research and train young apprentices who have chosen to learn from them. On the whole, they often abstract from the moral and political development of their students and shape their intellectual formation toward the requirements of the specialized disciplines. The faculty at a university largely do what they do in the service of their disciplines. This is, undeniably, a noble and important enterprise, but it is not the proper mission of the college.[8]

Colleges, by contrast, exist to inform, enlarge, refine, and discipline the minds of their students. The ordered personal and intellectual development of their students is their central concern. Although the college celebrates and contributes to the advancement of knowledge, it is not essentially organized to promote this specific good. We are speaking of authentic colleges, now.

There are many legitimate goods that the college does not directly pursue, so that it may focus its energies on the critical good for which it is chiefly responsible. Liberal arts colleges are the last serious cultural institution we have that treats their students and faculty as citizens of a common world, and requires them to learn a common language and history with which to discuss and appraise what the world contains.[9] It insists that what we have in common intellectually is as important as what separates us into biologists, mathematicians, artists, and historians. It deliberately resists the deep tendency in our culture to emphasize specialized learning to the detriment of educational balance and a shared intellectual heritage. The defining voice of the college should always be raised for wholeness of mind and for intellectual and political community.[10] When the members of a university are most serious, they speak in the specialized language of their disciplines. But the authentic voice of the college is different. It is framed in a vocabulary and presumes a matrix of allusion and reference that all of its members share. A mutual fund of experience, knowledge, and values is essential to the college and its graduates. For the sake of specialized research and discovery, universities have had to abandon this collegiate ideal.

Today, liberal arts colleges are in retreat before the advance of the university. Even when the traditional rhetoric of liberal education has been preserved, the qualities of mind it once represented are becoming rarer. It is the specialized or scholarly intellect that we honor. The members of college faculties know this. They have been trained by masters in a discipline and have their own aspirations to intellectual distinction. Generally, they love their particular field of research and delight in students who show a special promise in their field. They devote precious hours to their scholarship, and often chafe at the obligations of the classroom when it diverts them from their deepest love. Teaching students with no desire to advance in their chosen field is seen as the price to be paid for the practice of their true profession. Even the most conscientious teachers see little dignity in preparing the young for their enduring political and cultural vocations and for membership in the global community of intellect. For most of them, the concepts these terms express are vague and indeterminate. What vocation, what community, what shared obligations and goods, are you talking about? The mindset of the university has thus obscured basic truths once held to be definitive for the college.

My purpose in these reflections is not to beat the dead horse of specialization. The members of a college faculty are properly expected to be specialists in a discipline or scholars in their field. But teaching college students and training future scholars are not the same activity.[11] Very few college students ever become permanent members of the college or university. Our colleges then must be consistent in opposing premature vocationalism. The specialized life of scholarship or scientific research is as much a vocation as medicine, law, engineering, or architecture. As liberal arts colleges do not directly educate women and men for the great public professions, so they do not educate them directly to be scholars or scientists. The very difficult task for teachers of the liberal arts is to identify and articulate the substantive core of their particular field that everyone ought to know now. What part of mathematics, biology, history, psychology, and poetry, for example, should be part of our common heritage today? There is no more important educational judgment that college teachers must make together.[12]

In college teaching, one moves in and out of different rhetorical stances. Sometimes, teachers speak from the standpoint of their particular discipline; at others, from the perspective of the more experienced adult who has learned with difficulty the complex ways of the world. In both cases, their intended audience remains the same, young people with whom they share a common world and to whom they want to transmit a common heritage. This dual mission requires college teachers to master two voices and often two languages: the voice of a specialist speaking to peers within a discipline, and the voice of liberally educated adults speaking to those who will soon be their peers within the broader arena of public life. Liberal education, without directly qualifying a person for any specific employment in life, is of singular value because it enriches and complements all of them.

The great contemporary danger to the college's integrity results from an unholy alliance among students, parents, and prospective employers dominated by premature vocational concerns, and compliant faculty whose ultimate allegiance is to the university model of learning. In their different ways, each group thinks of college as an intellectual marketplace that caters to private desire. Students often want to study what immediately interests them; faculty want to teach courses in their areas of research and to work closely with students whose interests resemble their own. A policy of educational *laissez-faire* often prevails. Faculty are willing to let students do their own thing, if students will grant them the same privilege. As a result, the college comes to resemble a permissive household, with parents and children going their own ways in the name of democracy, freedom, and consumer rights. In such a setting, no wonder talk of intellectual and civic community seems vapid.[13]

The faculty bear the chief responsibility for this serious confusion of ends. After all, they are the educators not the students. Wise faculty invariably *learn* much from their students, but they are not *educated* by them. If this unholy alliance of interests is to be broken, the faculty will have to disengage first. To do this, they must realize that laudable love of their chosen field of knowledge is not enough. There is no invisible hand in education, or in politics, to bring public order out of the unrelenting pursuit of private interest. The liberal arts faculty, as a collective body, has an essential responsibility for the balanced development of all their students. It is foolish to pretend that this obligation can be discharged without requiring students and faculty to rise above their private and individual passions.

Let us agree, then, what liberal arts colleges are not. They are not mini-universities, intellectual marketplaces, or vocational training grounds. Each of these appealing substitutes emphasizes the private choices of

individuals and neglects to prepare them for their important public obligations. Liberal arts colleges, by contrast, are the final stage of public education. They exist to empower their students with the arts and virtues required
for living responsible lives, both public and personal. To set forth the right
standards of intellectual excellence, to educate with continual reference to
them, and to help all students meet them according to their capacities: that is
the true mission of a college.

There are three distinct but related goods that a liberal education seeks to
cultivate: to inform the mind with a common fund of knowledge and truth; to
discipline our native powers of intellect and speech until students become art-
ful in their exercise; to begin to transform knowledge and art into something
deeper, finer, and more personal, the human virtue traditionally called wisdom. We are not born with these attributes, nor do we acquire them routinely
as we develop with age. They are the precise fruit of liberal learning and the
specific goal of a liberal arts college.

We are no longer talking of Renaissance men or women.[14] As Bernard
Lonergan emphasized, the fund of human knowledge is far too great for any
individual to master all of it. Therefore, it is imperative that the faculty of a
college decide together what portion of that fund shall be held in common by
its graduates today. Since knowledge grows relentlessly in our culture, this
decision will need to be regularly revised in the light of cognitive advances
and corrections. Because the faculty of an authentic college belong to an
intellectual community that transcends their disciplinary differences, they
must reach these critical curricular decisions through shared discussion, dialogue and consent.

To identify the shifting boundaries of required knowledge is the proper task
of the whole faculty, but it is possible to articulate the epistemic domains in
which all students should be informed and literate: mathematics, natural science, the human sciences, critical history, and the creative arts with special
emphasis on the classic texts of Western and English poetry, history, and
literature. There should also be a shared critical awareness of our different
cultural traditions based on direct engagement with their great achievements
in painting, music, science, poetry, philosophy, and theology.[15] The cultural
assimilation of still living traditions serves a double end. It provides each student with an immediate experience of excellence under a variety of different
forms. And it secures for all members of the college a common field of meta-
phor and reference. Without this common fund of knowledge, both proposi-
tional and experiential, colleges are intellectual communities only in name.[16]

Since the late nineteenth century, the cognitive drift in the West has been
toward ever narrower communities of inquiry. This drift has been institution-
alized in the university and only weakly resisted by the college. It is therefore imperative that the faculty of a college deliberately resist that drift in

framing its curricular policy. This reversal of emphasis does not preclude the existence of departmental majors, although it is likely to circumscribe their imperial ambitions. In their last two years, students should strive for knowledge in depth of one particular field. Depth within the context of the college does not chiefly mean preparation for graduate study. Rather, it should mean a holistic understanding of one's chosen field or discipline: a knowledge of its history and development, mastery of its methods of inquiry and specialized vocabulary, concrete practice in working with and resolving its defining problems, an appreciation of its subordinate parts and their inter-connection, responsibility for its established results and foundational principles. Whether or not our students continue in graduate or professional studies, they should have a clear appreciation of how the global community of learning is presently organized. In our culture today, this sustained disciplinary focus prior to commencement is an essential part of their liberal education.

The utmost care must be taken to ensure that a restricted disciplinary concentration does not undermine the commitment to a common fund of knowledge. The best way to prevent this is to appoint a diverse teaching faculty whose educational allegiance to the mission of the college is as strong as their loyalty to specific departments. Departmental membership is a sign of specialized competence; membership in the comprehensive college faculty means that specialization does not exhaust a teacher's intellectual range nor define his/her educational mission. All the branches of liberal knowledge are represented in the college, but they are not isolated from one another. Because they form a diverse and dynamic whole, the teaching faculty must work together continually to understand their inter-dependence and complementarity. To do this, they must participate in a sustained and deepening conversation on the intelligible relations among their disciplines and on the bearing of their particular field on a common curricular policy. It is futile and unconvincing to ask our students to master a common fund of knowledge unless they witness all their teachers contributing to it and drawing from it. Students will only really believe in the rhetoric of intellectual community when they see that the faculty actually constitute one.[17]

The faculty should be able to talk fruitfully with one another because they share an acquired set of intellectual and discursive powers. The traditional name for these shared powers is the liberal arts. Students at a college should be apprentices in these arts of which their teachers are expected to be masters. Historically, these were the arts of language: grammar, rhetoric and logic (*the trivium*), and the arts of measurement: arithmetic, geometry, music, and astronomy (the *quadrivium*). It may be helpful to insert here an important historical reflection in order to clarify the special challenges facing liberal education today.

Let's begin by comparing the different social and cultural contexts in which liberal education has been considered essential to human well-being. The ancient Greek and Roman societies, where liberal education began, were predicated on human inequality. In particular, the socio-economic inequality between masters and slaves, and the political inequality between men and women. There also existed in these societies, as in ours, a critical distinction between the private and public spheres of human activity. In the private realm of the household (the *oikos*), masters ruled over their slaves, and husbands ruled over their wives and children. The public realm in free political societies, known then as republics, was understood, by contrast, to be a sphere of civic equality, based not on coercion or rule, but on discursive persuasion and informed rational argument among peers. The political intercourse of free citizens with free citizens that constitutes the *bios politikos*, the political life.

But for masters and husbands accustomed to private coercion and rule, to meet the high demands of a free and vibrant public life, they had to be liberally educated. That meant concretely, they had to be *freed from* the private mentality of inequality, rule and self-interest; and to be *freed for* the public liberty of effective and responsible citizenship ordered to the well-being of the whole political community. In unequal societies, where only the few are free, liberal education was literally intended *for free men* (male masters, not slaves or women), and *to free men*, that is to transform private rulers into free, equal, and responsible citizens.

Both continuity and difference persisted, therefore, when the historic shift slowly occurred to genuinely democratic societies, where there are no slaves, where women are justly recognized as the domestic and civic equals of men, and where nearly every adult person must meet both economic and political obligations. The discontinuity exists in the gradual, difficult, and still unfinished emergence of a shared social, cultural, and political structure predicated on human equality, where all democratic citizens are granted the same rights, privileges, and responsibilities. But continuity exists in the abiding contrast between the private realm, based on self-interest and care for one's own, and the public realm based on the comprehensive and enduring well-being, the common good, of the inclusive and evolving democratic society. Continuity also exists in the continuing need for a liberal education to transform privately oriented men and women into effective, persuasive, and public spirited citizens.

Clearly, the challenges facing liberal education are greater now than ever before, because today its distinctive benefits are needed by all citizens, regardless of their particular social and economic circumstances. For the formal equality of citizens on which political democracies are based, coexists with very high levels of racial, socio-economic, and educational inequalities that make the reliable transition to shared and effective public liberty especially difficult. And this challenge is particularly strong in capitalist economies and cultures, where the deliberate pursuit of self-interest extends to nearly every sphere of life, including the intellectual, moral, political, and religious. The very cultural spheres deliberately designed to summon human beings to transcend self-interest for the sake of intrinsic goods common to us all.

An instructive sense of historical difference also extends to the liberal arts themselves. How should we articulate those traditional arts today? They include the power to read intelligently and to write and speak clearly in one's native language; the power to read with enjoyment and to converse fluently in at least one foreign language; the mastery of basic mathematical operations including those of statistics and the calculus; and an understanding of their critical use in the natural and social sciences. They also include the capacity to construct, analyze, and appraise complex arguments; heightened powers of observation, appreciation, and criticism in the creative arts; sensitivity to bias in its different forms; practice in the formation and confirmation of scientific hypotheses; and the ability to integrate different types of knowledge without blurring their differences in method and vocabulary.

It is naive to think that human beings are naturally articulate. Stammering seems to be our native form of eloquence (Eugene O'Neill).[18] We need to be liberally educated before we can appreciate the challenging symbolism of literature and art, the conceptual distinctions regularly framed by the mind, the canons of evidence required for critical judgments, and the courage and practical wisdom demanded by responsible choice. The cultivation of these complementary powers cannot be left to nature or to chance. In speaking of the arts, Aristotle makes the crucial point. "Those things we have to learn before we can do them, we learn by doing them."[19] We learn to write and speak clearly by writing and speaking under sustained critical guidance. We learn how to understand and evaluate responsibly by exercising our native powers under supportive and critical supervision. We strive to become masters of our creative and intellectual abilities by regularly encountering the finest examples of these powers at work, and then by testing ourselves against these exemplary models.

When we read Shakespeare, we learn disciplined freedom in the use of language. When we study Plato's dialogues, we learn what freedom of thought actually means. When we carefully examine a Rembrandt painting, we discover what a freely trained hand can do. When we review and reconstruct a Euclidean proof, we learn the beauty and power of deductively ordered argument. The regular encounter with selected models of excellence, from different historical traditions, teaches us that we are not essentially free to do with our minds, hands, tongues, or spirits what we most deeply desire. In Lonergan's terms: the essential freedom of human beings is necessary but not sufficient for their effective freedom. Liberal education deliberately engages our essential freedom for the sake of developing our effective freedom, both personal and public.[20]

In Modernity, the basic models of human freedom have either been *negative*, emphasizing *freedom from* the Roman Trinity of religion, tradition and authority, or *hyperbolic*, implying that we are naturally self-sufficient and independent when it comes to discovering and doing what is right, and achieving what is good.[21] But when we take seriously the situated nature of human beings, their life-long struggle for greater maturity, and their clear dependence on the teaching and cooperation of others, then we recognize that effective freedom only develops through uniting the common education we receive from others, however imperfect, with our own sustained efforts at self-corrective learning. In education, the "we" properly comes before the "I," but the free developing subject gradually emerges through the dedicated teaching community to shape, in collaboration with our peers, an enlarged community that is hopefully wiser, more just and more inclusive.[22]

The very best things place the greatest demands on us. In doing so, they awaken the latent demands we want to place upon ourselves. This is the traditional rhythm of liberal education:

> Intensive ordered engagement with the best in mathematics, science, history, literature, the arts and philosophy, under the guidance of dedicated adults who know what is best even if they cannot fully replicate it, until these sustained and humbling encounters arouse our personal desire to participate in these activities as equals.

Criticism of liberal education comes from several different directions. It is therefore important to insist that the liberal arts are concrete and verifiable, that there are specific exercises and programs of study that foster them, and that there are recognized standards for measuring their attainment. The substantive faith of a liberal arts college has a definite normative content: there is a common fund of knowledge, jointly defined, reviewed, and revised by the faculty, for which all our students are responsible. There are cultivated human powers of attention, understanding, articulation, reflection, and discernment no liberal arts graduate is at liberty to exclude or omit.

But the mastery of knowledge and the cultivation of the liberal arts, however important, fall short of a college's highest hopes. Colleges want their students ultimately to be wise and good. Wisdom and goodness are not virtues that can be required, nor even sometimes ascertained. Yet, without them liberal arts graduates lack what is necessary to give grandeur to knowledge and nobility to art. A college's final purpose is the cultivation of virtue, particularly the intellectual virtues insofar as they deepen and heighten moral character. At its best, liberal education is a form of ethical inquiry in which the basic human purposes are examined and evaluated, and the criteria with which to evaluate them are made explicit.

Liberal arts colleges are not neutral between justice and partisanship, public service and selfishness, responsible speech and action, and thoughtless, deceptive or self-serving words and deeds. Still, the chief support a college faculty can offer for these values is through the quality of their daily lives. Since the time of Socrates, the most persuasive argument for high moral principles and demanding human values has been their informing presence in the conduct of ordinary men and women.

Although it is appropriate to measure a liberal arts college by the moral and intellectual character of its graduates, it is difficult to say precisely how the liberal arts make human beings better. One way to clarify the connection is by thinking carefully about adult morality. Most adult conduct is habitual rather than reflective and deliberate. We spend far more time speaking and doing than we do thinking and carefully deciding. But what we do and how we do it is influenced greatly by the quality of deliberation, which precedes our action and by the quality of remembrance that completes it. Both deliberation and remembrance are forms of practical thinking in which our awareness of time plays a critical role. Deliberation allows us to make our choices in the light of the deepest awareness of time we can achieve. Remembrance allows us to appraise judiciously the actions and outcomes to which our choices lead.

The depth and significance of an action are proportionate to the depth of temporal awareness that serves as its illuminating background. This important connection is illustrated in the medieval legend of a traveler who met three men engaged in a common task. When asked what he was doing, the first replied, "I am laying one brick upon another." The second answered, "I am shaping a wall." The third proudly declared, "I am building a cathedral." This ancient story reminds us that the meaning and importance of an activity for an agent largely depends on the temporal and cultural horizons of which the agent is actually aware.

In both our habitual activities and our weightiest choices, most of us are victims of the silent tyranny exercised by the present and immediate.[23] We often fail to appreciate the depth of our decisions and actions, because we lack awareness of their causal antecedents and consequents, or we exaggerate their significance because we lack a critical personal or historical scale against which to measure them. Either way, we act irresponsibly because we misjudge the actual worth of what we and others are doing.

Every culture, but particularly our own at this critical stage in our history, needs respected institutions that correct our bias toward the unexamined, the familiar, the fashionable, the parochial, and self-serving. This is the proper function of the Supreme Court and a genuinely independent judiciary in the constitutional balance of powers. Liberal arts colleges ought to play a parallel role in the formation of young adults. Parental pressure for career choice, the highly advertised models of "success," and our natural desire to escape uncertainty about the future, all need to be steadily resisted by an enlarged sense of time and significance, so that our identity defining personal choices can be reached and revised with maximum integrity.

Wisdom is the slowly emerging fruit of sustained intellectual and moral development. It is this balanced growth of individual persons and citizens within free and responsible communities that is the aim of liberal education. Liberal arts colleges strive to complete the temporally limited but critical process of human education that begins with our birth and culminates in our intellectual, moral, and political coming of age. In their moments of truth, colleges ultimately measure themselves by the emerging wisdom of their graduates and faculty.

As a student and teacher of the liberal arts for over sixty years, I deeply believe that this is the heart of the matter.

NOTES

1. Some of the important works that have shaped my thinking about liberal education include: Hannah Arendt's *Between Past and Future*; Aristotle's *Ethics and Politics*; Augustine's *Confessions;* Andrew Delbanco's *College*; Werner Jaeger's *Paideia*; Lonergan's *Insight and Method in Theology*; Newman's *Idea of a University*; Plato's *Dialogues*; Charles Taylor's *Sources of the Self* and *A Secular Age*; Alexis de Tocqueville's *Democracy in America*; Joseph Tussman's *An Experiment at Berkeley*; and Alfred North Whitehead's *The Aims of Education.*

2. As always, I draw on a broad range of Lonergan's work, but especially *Verbum, Insight, Method in Theology and Topics in Education.*

3. See Hannah Arendt's "The Crisis in Education," chapter 5 in *Between Past and Future*, where she clarifies the important distinction between education and learning.

4. I'm struck by how often contemporary defenders of a college education focus on its economic function of "credentialing" the young for subsequent employment opportunities. Because nearly all democratic citizens must work for a living, preparation for an emerging career is a legitimate educational concern. But it is a clear sign of our narrow understanding of a college's mission that we have allowed the economic perspective to supplant the intellectual, moral, political, and cultural aims of a liberal education. See chapter 7, "The Cultural Struggle for American Democracy."

5. In a capitalist culture, like ours, the important and clarifying distinction between necessary, useful, and liberal goods is consistently forgotten or ignored.

6. We also fail regularly to articulate the full range of public goods and responsibilities essential to an authentic community, as well as the specific forms of knowledge and virtue required to achieve them consistently.

7. See Joseph Tussman, *An Experiment at Berkeley* (New York: Oxford University Press, 1969).

8. See Lonergan's important distinction between the realms and stages of cognitive meaning in *Method in Theology*, 85–99.

9. Hannah Arendt articulates the civic obligations of all mature citizens in these terms: to know, love, and accept responsibility for the world. See *Between Past and Future*, 188–95.

10. See Lonergan's important contrast in the third stage of meaning between "seeking the whole in knowledge" versus "the whole of knowledge."

11. So many of our errors in the theory and practice of education result from taking the part for the whole in confusing complementary both/ands with exclusive either/ors; the part for the whole.

12. See Lonergan's important distinction between Classicism and contemporary Historical Mindedness in *A Second Collection*, 1–9. A distinction particularly relevant now, as the range of factual knowledge regularly expands, and as historical knowledge leads us to re-examine periodically the models of cultural excellence we affirm for our students.

13. In discussing liberal education, it is critical to distinguish different senses of the term "liberal." The meaning of "liberal," in the case of the liberal arts or liberal goods, is radically different from its use in reference to classical *liberal* economic theory, based on *laissez-faire* and the invisible hand. At the root of this contrast are very different understandings of human freedom. See chapter 3 of this work.

14. For the limited relevance today of the Renaissance ideal of "universal knowledge," see *A Second Collection*, 181–82.

15. Just as the faculty in developing and revising the curriculum in the empirical sciences must take account of important cognitive developments in those fields, it must also be sensitive and alert to provincialism and cultural bias in the arts and humanities. That bias can take different forms, but especially the exclusion of important texts and achievements by women, African Americans and members of non-European ethnic groups. Finding a flexible balance between conservation and change is essential to sound curricular formation in all the relevant fields of study.

16. Joseph Tussman trenchantly criticizes the narrow focus of public faculty debates at Berkeley, contrasting the intense communal dialogue required to develop an appropriate undergraduate curriculum, with the narrow absorption of his peers in securing faculty parking options on campus. Though Tussman exaggerates for effect, his critical point is clearly worth making.

17. Quite often, the power of concrete examples to inspire devotion to a challenging ideal is more persuasive than the repeated resort to verbal exhortation, however well meant. I know this from the example of dedicated teachers as an undergraduate student, and the related example of responsible statesmen as an engaged citizen.

18. See Eugene O'Neill's remarkable play, *Long Day's Journey Into Night*, for this humbling reflection of Edmond Tyrone.

19. See Aristotle's *Nicomachean Ethics*, Book II, 1103a 35–36.

20. For Lonergan's important distinction between essential and effective freedom, see *Insight*, 619–24.

21. Hannah Arendt introduces the important historical and cultural theme of The Roman Trinity, religion, tradition, and authority in chapter 3, "What Is Authority?" of *Between Past and Future*.

22. In the early stages of education, the developing subject "belongs pre-critically" to his/her family and community. But liberal education is intended to transform "pre-critical" to "critical belonging," in which intentional subjects become able to distinguish the merits from the limitations of the various groups to which they give their allegiance. For a more detailed account of "critical belonging," see Michael McCarthy's *Toward a Catholic Christianity*, xii–xxi.

23. One of the great weaknesses of contemporary American culture are its serious and repeated failures of memory. The tyranny of the present largely depends on a prior forgetfulness of the past. But as Hannah Arendt wisely reminds us, "Memory is the faculty of depth." For the past is not dead, it is not even past (William Faulkner).

Chapter 5

The Critical Appropriation of Traditions

Reflections of a Teacher

Hannah Arendt states the task of the teacher in these terms. By nature, the teacher is a mediator who connects the young, the newcomers, with the older and larger world they are about to enter. As a representative of our common world, the teacher addresses three imperatives to his or her students. Know the world! Love the world! Accept your share of responsibility for its well-being and survival! The three imperatives are interdependent, for you cannot be responsible for the world unless you know it (in all its greatness and misery); and you will not sustain that responsibility, or bear it gracefully under pressure, unless you love it and have allied yourself with its uncertain future.[1]

I begin with this reflection on teaching because my concerns in this essay have their origin in my own experience as a student and teacher of the liberal arts. It has always been difficult for young people to know, love, and bear responsibility for the world. But I fear that this difficulty has increased in the fifty-seven years since I began to teach and work with college students. This is not chiefly because the world has grown more complex in that time, and thus somewhat harder to know (although I believe this has occurred). Rather, what troubles me is that it has become harder for my students and our children to love and assume responsibility for the world, to take their place as mature adults within it. Adults who recognize that an important part of their dignity consists in their shared obligations to the world and to the generations who shall succeed them as its inhabitants.

I connect this increasing personal difficulty with a more general cultural phenomenon that I shall refer to as "the Modern Predicament."[2] The title of this essay, "The Critical Appropriation of Traditions," suggests one important way of responding to that predicament, one way in which teachers, like myself, can sustain their own allegiance to the world, and, at the same time, assist their students in assuming their rightful positions within it

THE CRITICAL APPROPRIATION OF TRADITIONS

"All our predecessors render us the double service of hitting off the truth for us or of missing the mark, and so challenging us to get to the root of the matter ourselves."[3]

Aristotle, *De Anima*

Since the end of the first World War, cultural commentators in the West have spoken recurrently of a crisis of modernity. Because the idiom of *crisis* has become stale from overuse, there is an understandable temptation to dismiss their remarks as hyperbolic. I urge you to resist that temptation, for I do not find it a hyperbole to say that the present condition of the world is critical. The English term *crisis* derives from a Greek verb *krinein*, meaning to decide or to judge; the reason it is appropriate to speak of a crisis in modernity is that we now live at a decisive period in the modern era that clearly calls for critical reflection and judgment. This crisis can be discerned at two interdependent levels; the first is cultural and the second institutional. The culture of a community develops, preserves, and transmits the central ideas and normative standards the community requires for its self-understanding and appraisal. It articulates the beliefs and commitments that inform the fundamental institutions of an historically unified people. When the underlying meanings and values of a community become insecure, its basic institutions, the family, the church, the authority of government, the security and military services, the economic order, and the essential mission of its schools, colleges, and universities are invariably at risk. By definition, a cultural crisis is a crisis of education, for a central purpose of education is to articulate, refine, revise, and transmit the cultural resources that give a people their collective identity. According to Charles Taylor and Michael Polanyi, the roots of our present crisis go very deep, because they are located in constitutive elements of modernity itself.[4]

For our purposes in this chapter, I shall concentrate on three essential features of the distinctively *modern* outlook: our moral aspirations, our historical consciousness, our passion for criticism. Let me begin with a few brief words about each. The unprecedented moral aspirations of modernity can be articulated most concisely in the declared purposes of the French Revolution: liberty for *all* people; equality among *all* people; fraternity with *all* people. The modern ideal of liberty as autonomy, self-determining subjectivity, receives political expression in our contemporary insistence on universal human rights. The modern ideal of equality is distrustful of all inherited forms of hierarchy, and tends to view the exercise of authority in any form as an overt or covert mode of domination. The modern ideal of fraternity means that all human persons are responsible for each other's well-being, however spatially distant their dwelling places may be on this earth. I am my sister's and brother's keeper whether she lives in Somalia or Syria, whether he lives in Myanmar, Yemen, or Ukraine.

A second decisive feature of the modern identity is its unprecedented historical and global consciousness. We are aware that the earth contains many different co-existing cultures that are rooted in opposing and often hostile historical traditions. We also know that respect for this cultural diversity is an important way of showing respect to the individual persons for whom those cultures constitute a spiritual home. At the same time, we recognize the great difference in assumptions and aspirations that separate the cultures and institutions of the past from those of the present. We know that slavery was a matter of course in the ancient Greek *polis*, but that all signs of human subjugation have rightly become intolerable to our contemporaries. Our global and historical consciousness deprives us of cultural innocence. Cultural pluralism inherently problematizes; it makes us question whether our own beliefs and values are defensible; it makes us wonder how posterity will judge our deepest convictions and attachments.[5]

The third defining trait of modernity is the stern critical passions we moderns have embraced since the seventeenth century. Since its advent at the dawn of modern science, our passion for criticism has taken several forms: the radical hyperbolic doubt of Descartes, the decoding of spiritual and cultural ideologies by Marx and Freud, the post-modern passion for subversive genealogies initiated by Nietzsche, the comprehensive suspicion that, as Moses Herzog, one of Saul Bellow's heroes, states it, "the spiritual and moral life, the so called higher life, is ultimately a racket."[6] According to Charles Taylor, the only conception of the human being able to survive this radical self-scrutiny is an anthropology based on appetite, *libido*, the unrelenting drive for power and self-interest. The lowest and basest dimension of the soul in Plato's famous tri-partite picture in the *Republic* has become the defining image of the human in our age of unmasking.[7]

But there are deep problems with this exclusively appetitive and aggressive conception of human nature. First, it suppresses or distorts the full reality of the human spirit. Because of its critical desire not to conceal human violence, sexual passion, and the will to power, it casts suspicion on our native intelligence and reasonableness, and our intrinsic longing for a broad range of genuine goods. This reductive account is also dangerous at a deeper level, for it is evidently unable to sustain the full weight of modern moral aspirations. The cultural challenges set by our exigent moral ideals and our heightened sensitivity to pluralism would be rigorous enough under the best of historical conditions. But the cult of suspicion engendered by our critical adversarial culture threatens the very manner in which we transmit and appropriate our complex cultural inheritance. To the extent that the acids of suspicion erode our allegiance to the depth of this inheritance, they tend to throw us back on the very untutored appetites and emotions that an authentic culture seeks to redeem and transform.[8]

Faced with this dilemma, our contemporaries seem drawn in three opposing directions. Some seek a return to a pre-modern, pre-critical epistemic paradise antecedent to the advent of modern suspicion. Others see no credible way of turning back from the abyss revealed by deconstructive criticism. If the relentless modern critique should deprive our culture and its institutions of their legitimacy, this is simply the price we shall have to pay for unwelcome truth.

For myself, I find both of these cultural postures unsatisfying. We *cannot* return to a pre-modern world even if we should want to; nor can we live as authentic human beings in a climate of radical distrust. What we require, instead, is a critical appropriation of the three great historical traditions, Pre-Modern, Modern, and Post-Modern, that have shaped the contemporary culture of the West. Such an appropriation would enable us to acknowledge the achievements and limitations of each of these periods. It would also confirm that the "modern predicament" is rooted in a deeper problem than unsparing adversarial criticism. I am referring to the pervasive modern unease about the past, about our human situatedness in history, about our dependence on intellectual and cultural traditions that we did not create or construct.

The new insights generated by critical appropriation will also require us to modify important aspects of our contemporary moral ideals. The neat conjunction of liberty with unlimited autonomy, and the equally neat opposition between authority and equality, will need to be carefully revised. The aspiration to universal fraternity and sorority should be thoughtfully supported, but its plausibility depends on sources of moral energy and insight that the cult of suspicion has been unwilling to acknowledge and affirm. In the face of our "modern predicament," my considered recommendation as a teacher is blunt and direct: we need judiciously to make our own the full range of what has been transmitted to us by our predecessors. That is simply what the critical appropriation of traditions requires.[9]

PRE-CRITICAL BELONGING

Human belonging is the inescapable result of the conditions of our birth. Each of us is born into antecedent orders of meaning and value that we did not create. Our condition at birth is *non-voluntary* rather than *involuntary*. We do not choose the numerous givens of our existence, but we become able as we mature to acknowledge, accept and, to some degree, revise them. As Hannah Arendt reminds us, we are born into a world with others, to whom we are joined through webs of association that endure through time.[10] The associations to which we belong by birth are of different kinds: they include associations of intimacy and ancestry like the family, civic associations like the body politic, public orders of knowledge, technological competence and work, structures of education, and communities of worship. From the beginning of life till its end, our personal identity, our unique subjectivity, is rooted in nature and history. We constitutively belong to nature and history; they are among the defining conditions of our humanity.

This fact of primordial belonging has important and enduring implications. The human associations into which we are born are invariably orders of education and culture. Like every cultural agency, they transform our original biological nature into a second human nature. As you probably know, the etymology of *culture* is Latin. For the Romans, *cultura* meant to cultivate; originally the land, as in *agri-cultura*, and eventually the powers of the human spirit. A human culture cultivates the intellectual, moral, political, and spiritual character of a people; it shapes their common identity and purpose. How does it achieve this critical formative task? By cultivating ideas, opinions and convictions; shared emotions, aspirations, and manners; a communal sense of what is and is not important. Alexis de Tocqueville called these shared habits of thought and discourse, of affective response and evaluation, "habits of the heart."[11]

This was also the name Robert Bellah and his associates gave to their groundbreaking study of contemporary American culture. Every developed culture embodies a vision of the human being and the human good, a conception of the full humanity to which we commonly aspire. It also embodies a vision of human community, a rough understanding of how we might live together responsibly in freedom and justice.

In our early years, many of us participate in this formative process with humility and gratitude. As Michael Polanyi has argued, all cultural transmission presupposes the learner's tacit affiliation with the teaching community.[12] An implicit trust in authority is essential to human learning, especially the learning of languages that play such a major role in our highly literate modern cultures. But our tacit affiliation with authority does not end in childhood. It is a necessary condition of all successful apprenticeship, whether it occurs in the arts or sciences, in religion, or in philosophy. Aristotle put the essential point concisely: those things we need to learn before we can do them, we learn by doing them.[13] That is, by intelligently imitating the example of recognized models in whom we place confidence. This implicit reliance on authority, and on the historical traditions from which authority derives, continues long into adulthood.

Even in the empirical sciences, the amount of knowledge that any individual can justify from directly available evidence can never be large. Science, like the other great human practices, depends heavily on belief, and belief itself depends on a basic trust in the credibility and integrity of other persons.[14]

It is important to acknowledge, therefore, without equivocation, that this dependence on authority, this pre-critical acceptance of tradition and belief, is not irrational, but indispensable to the exercise of rationality. It is not an obstacle to human freedom, but a necessary condition of becoming free. In all authentic education, genuine authority does not depend on blind obedience to others, but on a shared recognition of the relevant inequality of knowledge and competence between teachers and learners. Michael Polanyi's insistence on our original pre-critical or a-critical affiliation with the agencies of culture is strongly confirmed in the work of Hans Georg Gadamer. Gadamer insists that pre-critical belonging is the primordial condition of human existence. In fact, it precedes and enables the eventual exercise of critical judgment by the discerning adult. If the capacity for independent thought and judgment is one of the great marks of human autonomy, then autonomy itself depends on the prior acceptance of authority and tradition, and not on their systemic rejection.[15]

To this point in my argument, I have emphasized the great advantages that flow from our condition of historical belonging. But these advantages co-exist with an equally inescapable set of cultural dangers. Even the most genuine cultures transmit to their members an uneven legacy of greatness and wretchedness. Every human community is marked by both insight and blindness; and none is immune from the threat of systemic exclusion due to parochial prejudice or illegitimate distributions of power. Cultural claims to authority may be unfounded, as Plato argued in the *Gorgias*, insisting there on the critical distinction between the true and counterfeit arts. Given the unrelenting dynamism of modern societies, cultural traditions, once vital and enabling, may no longer be adequate to the exigencies of the present. There is also the mounting problem of cultural pluralism and the insecurity we feel about resolving important cultural conflicts without begging the question in our own favor.

For all of these reasons, contemporary dynamic and self-critical cultures are in a constant struggle for their lives. They either secure or fail to elicit the affection and allegiance of their younger members. If they are to remain vital and effective, their children, the newcomers, must personally accept their vision and values, be willing to preserve and augment their ideals, and in the ultimate test be prepared to sacrifice and die for them. The failure of cultures to secure this allegiance becomes evident in the unsatisfied hungers of those who belong to them, in their alienation and estrangement from the common vision of the good and from the existing norms of human cooperation.

The cultural phenomenon of personal alienation is greatly intensified in modern societies. Whether revolutionary or reformist, modern societies seek continually to transform themselves in accord with their ideals. According to Michael Polanyi, four coefficients of allegiance bind the members of a complex political association together: cultural consensus, group loyalty, economic cooperation, and civic power.[16] These coefficients are all less secure in the dynamic critical societies of the present than they were in the more static, tradition-based cultures of the past. Cultural consensus dissolves when inherited visions of the good, personal, and communal, no longer command shared agreement. Group loyalty and commitment may easily appear to be parochial and biased, serving narrow and partisan, rather than catholic and common interests. Economic conflicts between groups with opposing objectives frequently set the rich, the poor, and the middle class against each other. And civic power is no longer trusted when seen as the instrument of an exploitative ruling class, or a coercive minority. In the limit case, a defiant rebellion emerges against illegitimate cultural ideals used to defend systemic patterns of violence and domination.

No culture can guarantee its immunity from this illicit pattern of failure, abuse, and ideology. And yet, the familiar pattern of cultural alienation remains inherently ambiguous. It is a mistake to assume that the posture of personal disaffection is always justified. Though it may spring from warranted protest against cultural and civic illegitimacy, it may also emerge from individual unwillingness to accept a legitimate culture's authentic demands. Given the intensity of modern moral aspirations, it may often derive from an uncritical idealism in which support for real but neglected goods is believed to require the denial and suppression of others that are equally genuine.[17]

Pre-modern societies tended to look to the *past* as their primary source of guidance and direction. This was particularly true of medieval culture with its explicit dependence on the inherited Roman Trinity of religion, tradition, and authority.[18] A decisive shift occurred in modern societies when they began to appraise themselves in terms of an unrealized future ideal that was often eschatological in nature. In the modern West, these normative ideals take several forms: scientific, philosophical, moral, political, and economic.

To take just five examples, one from each of these interdependent realms. Galileo's ideal of a *mathesis universalis*, a single, comprehensive, mathematical science of nature, a unified science of being and truth. Descartes's ideal of objectively certain demonstrative knowledge (science) invulnerable to radical doubt. Kant's ideal of a universal moral kingdom, the self-legislating kingdom of ends. The French Revolutionary ideal of a unified civic republic based on the liberty, equality, and fraternity of all its citizens. Marx's transformation of the French Revolutionary vision into a universal classless society.

To fulfill these exigent modern ideals, the leading thinkers of modernity advocated a critical emancipation from the cultural inheritance of the past. Descartes sought scientific certainty through the practice of hyperbolic doubt; Kant sought moral objectivity and rigor through the autonomy of pure practical reason; the Jacobins sought revolutionary justice by eradicating the inherited structures of the *ancien regime*. It has been decisive for the history of modernity that the paradigmatic strategy for overcoming cultural, intellectual, and civic alienation was through deliverance from the inherited forms of participatory belonging. This strategy is the critical emancipatory counterpart to the positive modern ideal of autonomy, or self-determining freedom.

In his *Discourse on Method*, Descartes articulates the distinctively modern ideal of the autonomous rational self, the free and independent thinker, liberated from all forms of inherited belonging, natural and historical. But the ideal of rational autonomy was not confined to epistemology; it became the basis of modern moral and political theory as well. Kant made the foundational principle of ethics the autonomy of pure practical reason. For Kant, the autonomy of the rational will is the ontological ground of human dignity, the compelling reason we should treat every rational being as an end in him or herself. The distinctively modern forms of political theory also rest on the principle of autonomy. This is evident in the various versions of the social contract theory where the state of nature is presented as the original condition of humankind. According to the contractual fiction of modern liberal theory, all civil society, all institutional order, all moral and political obligations are only binding if they derive from the voluntary consent of an originally free natural being.

It is crucial to recognize how this early modern understanding of autonomy reverses the priority claims we made for pre-critical belonging. We have argued that our initial acceptance of tradition and authority is necessary for the development and exercise of critical reason. But the modern ideal of pure individual reason, historically unsituated reason, stands that humbling conclusion on its head. According to Descartes, only pure individual reason can actually be autonomous; and reason can only be pure if it is first purified of nature and history, liberated from all sources of inherited belief and conviction it does not completely control. In the scientific method proposed by Descartes, the first operation of reason is radical doubt, the decision to put the natural and historical givens of existence into question unless they can meet the strict test of indubitability.[19] Under the enduring spell of Descartes, distrust rather than acceptance, suspicion rather than faith, became the hallmarks of the educated modern mind. But liberated reason, so construed, is ahistorical and unsituated. It achieves its vaunted autonomy only through a radical divorce from the past, a divorce that excludes authority, belief, and tradition as legitimate sources of truth.[20]

I want to emphasize that the Enlightenment conception of reason was not exclusively critical. Constructive rational activity was intended to occur on the secure ground critical reason had cleared. For Descartes, this meant the construction of a universal science of nature on a foundation of indubitable truths. For Kant, it meant universal laws of obligation binding on all rational creatures. For the Jacobins and later for the Bolsheviks, it meant the construction of a perfect, fraternal republic once the rubbish of earlier history had been cleared away.

With the onset of the nineteenth century and the restoration of the Bourbon monarchy in France, we enter a new phase in the modern story. This second stage of modernity is deeply influenced by philosophical romanticism and by the Romantic critique of Enlightenment ideals. Both Marx and Freud, two of the great nineteenth century "masters of suspicion," are intensely affected by the romantic movement. But their acceptance of romantic themes and insights does not lead them to reject the Enlightenment commitment to critical and constructive rationality. One reason for the continuing appeal of these thinkers in our own time is that they combine both of the great modern cultural traditions in their thought (The Enlightenment and Romanticism). Still, this warranted emphasis on continuity with their modern predecessors should not be overstated. Both Marx and Freud turn the modern strategy of radical critique against itself. A common target for their critical energies is the Cartesian and Kantian ideal of pure reason. Freud and Marx are united in their intention to resituate reason within nature and history. Human reason, as they conceive it, is immersed in the cycles of productive and reproductive life, in the violence and conflicts of history, in the passion of sexuality, and the drives of aggressive self-interest. For both, human reason may still be powerful, but it is certainly never pure.

While Marx and Freud are openly critical of the Enlightenment picture of autonomous individual reason, they do not want to return to pre-modern cultural traditions. If anything, they only intensify the critical modern passion against the past. Both of them tend to view Western art, religion, philosophy, politics, and morality in a very negative light. For Marx, they are forms of cultural ideology used to justify economic exploitation or to pacify class-based resistance to it. For Freud, they express sublimated fantasies and

illusions, the false consolations of immature people unable to endure the bitter truths of reality. Both Marx and Freud mount this severe critique of the
past in the name of a specifically Enlightenment ideal, the ideal of objective
science. According to Freud, among the leading modern cultural practices,
only empirical science can escape the charge of offering false consolation,
because its defining truths are singularly unwelcome to the human psyche. As
examples of unwelcome truth, Freud offers these historic modern reversals
of classical thought. With his revolutionary heliocentric theory, Copernicus
deprived us of the consoling illusion that we humans exist at the center of
the cosmic drama. With his evolutionary theory of human ancestry, Darwin
deprived us of the biblical illusion that we are made in the image and like-
ness of the transcendent Creator God. And Freud himself, with his radical
depth psychology deprived us of the Cartesian illusion that we are the rational
masters of our own souls. In Freud's holistic appraisal, modern science is
the only recognized cultural practice completely in the service of the reality
principle.[21]

Marx is even more quintessentially modern than Freud. In Marx's thought
and practice, all aspects of the modern identity are connected: its unprecedented moral passions, its historical and global consciousness, its critical
thirst for unmasking. We noted earlier the modern tendency to measure existing societies in the light of an eschatological future. Marx's political ideal of
a universal classless society, free from all exploitation and ideology, and free
for unrestricted self-defining subjectivity is a classic instance of this pattern.
But Marx insists that this culminating historical *telos* will not come to pass
through reliance on spiritual and moral imperatives and aspirations. His critical passion requires that the utopian Socialist ideal be realized through natural
and historical forces and laws invulnerable to radical doubt. Therefore, he
relies on the very competitive material interests that have made previous history a locus of class struggle, eventually to produce the classless society. It
is natural and historical necessity that will generate freedom; it is the most
intense historical conflict that will culminate in justice.

Freud tends to view Marx's historical eschatology as yet another form of
consolatory illusion. He opposes his own tragic sense of life to Marx's ultimate
utopian optimism; and he argues against Marx, and the entire Revolutionary
tradition, that the moral aspirations of modernity are extravagant. For Freud,
we are able, with great difficulty, to increase human liberty and fraternity, and
we can reduce unnecessary forms of inequality. But we cannot realistically
hope for a classless society that embodies the French Revolutionary ideals.
The constraints of nature, civilized society, and our own psychological constitution are in ineradicable conflict with those historical illusions.[22]

Although Marx and Freud were deeply critical thinkers, they remained
committed to the Enlightenment ideals of critical reason, science, and

objectivity. In every context of struggle, they executed their passionate critical activity in the name of truth. In this respect, they differ significantly from Friedrich Nietzsche, the other great "master of suspicion" with whom they are often closely identified.[23] Nietzsche inaugurates a new phase in the modern project of unmasking by turning his critical passion, the subversive power of the negative, on the most deeply held Enlightenment values: truth, objectivity, science, and disinterested reason. In Nietzsche, the school of suspicion founded by Descartes has produced its most exceptional pupil. He contends that the Enlightenment's cultural norms all have their origin in an unacknowledged will to power; that scientific rationality is not an agency of historical freedom, but a new form of concealed domination. The Nietzschean critique of modern science as yet another variant of ideology is perhaps the most distinctive feature of post-modern thought. It receives expression in thinkers as different as Richard Rorty and Michel Foucault, and in the general post-modern opposition to epistemology, the theory of knowledge.

Freud consistently honored science for its unwavering commitment to truth and the reality principle. But according to Nietzsche and his post-modern successors, all forms of "truth" are inherently ideological; they are elaborately constructed fictions that serve as instruments of social power and control.[24] To substantiate this radical charge, the post-moderns resort to ingenious genealogies of suspicion modeled on Nietzsche's famous genealogical critique of morality. Drawing ironically on the narrative techniques of Marx and Freud, they offer a psychological and sociological critique of Enlightenment epistemic and moral values. Within the contemporary cult of unmasking, the Enlightenment's defining attachment to science, objectivity and truth is reconceived as a classic example of "unrecognized motivation serving unacknowledged purpose." [25](Alasdair MacIntyre)

After the deaths of Danton and Robespierre at the peak of the revolutionary terror, it was said of the French Revolution that it had devoured its own children. I am inclined to express similar sentiments about the modern revolution of suspicion. What is occurring, I believe, is an intellectual civil war at the heart of contemporary culture. The post-modern genealogists have turned the critical passions and historical consciousness of modernity on its own cognitive, moral, and political aspirations. Still, there appears to be a peculiar moral inversion at work in this assault.[26] For post-modern criticism seems *tacitly* to appeal to the very Enlightenment ideals it *explicitly* claims to deconstruct. After all, what gives the unmasking genealogies their revisionary power, if it is not their *implicit* claim to truth, their unstated contention that they have discovered a deeper level of motivation and purpose than their rivals have been able or willing to acknowledge. Both Michael Polanyi and Charles Taylor have emphasized the exceptional irony of the post-modern age. The very depth of modern critical suspicion has made its proponents reluctant to *acknowledge* their own intellectual and moral commitments.

The genealogists of suspicion have wanted no aspect of human selfishness and wretchedness to escape our attention. But they seem to have reached a limit where they are incapable of recognizing or accepting some of the most important and enduring sources of human greatness.[27]

Modernity has rightly emphasized the dangers of an uncritical acceptance of tradition. However, its own internal development has shown that a culture of unbridled suspicion is no less subject to abuse. What we presently require is to recover a position of sanity and balance between these divisive cultural extremes. To begin that recovery, let us humbly acknowledge that the human condition is a tangled knot of greatness and wretchedness.[28] Every human culture, tradition, institution, and practice is a center of achievement and limitation. The mark of a truly critical thinker or teacher is the capacity to distinguish wisely between achievement and limitation, and to remind us forcefully of whatever dimension of our being the culturally prevailing self-image tends to neglect. Pascal stated the pedagogical function of a good critic well. "When he exalts himself, I shall humble him; when he humbles himself, I shall exalt him." (*Pensées*, 130)

The critical point to emphasize is that there are two dangers to avoid here and not one. Cultural traditionalism and triumphalism are unjustified because they conceal the inevitable wretchedness of our historical inheritance; because they suppress the record of violence, bias, sin, illusion, and ideology that no human society or institution escapes. But the cult of suspicion is equally one-sided. In attempting to satisfy the stern critical passions of modernity, it has produced a very distorted image of the human being and the human past. The personal and communal sources of human greatness, our human desire for knowledge and truth, our enduring commitment to the genuinely good, our impressive capacity for self-transcendence, the powerful appeal of virtue and genuineness, these receive scant recognition in the appetitive and aggressive conception of the human person. Human life in general, our intellectual and cultural lives, in particular, are rarely well served by prolonged one-sidedness.[29] The Enlightenment strategy of radical emancipation and the post-modern fascination with subversive deconstruction have made us unduly suspicious of our entire cultural legacy. That suspicion affects all members of the contemporary world, but it strikes with particular force at our young. It tends to make them cynical, distrustful, and alienated just as they are about to assume the complex responsibilities of adults and citizens.[30]

It is here that the cultural responsibility of the teacher becomes so important. In representing and speaking for our common world, the teacher also represents the splendor and misery of its past. But we cannot represent what we do not actually understand, and we cannot responsibly transmit what we have not critically appropriated. As teachers, the critical appropriation and transmission of our different historical traditions is the heart of our calling. At this time, I believe, every aspect of our relation to the past is affected by *crisis*, by the need for thoughtful reflection, decision, and judgment. What do we need to retrieve from distortion, misrepresentation, or neglect after four centuries of radical doubt and suspicion? What persisting limitations of our cultures and societies is it time to acknowledge and remedy? In thinking critically about these questions, we need very different models from those offered by the "masters of suspicion" and their disciples.

I accept Gadamer's insight that participatory belonging is a constitutive feature of human existence. The real question is not *whether* we shall belong to received traditions, but in *what manner* we shall belong to them. Can we achieve a credible dialectic of belonging and distance, of allegiance and criticism, that preserves the riches and achievements of the past, but keeps us alert to their inevitable limitations? But the execution of such a nuanced dialectical strategy is in no way automatic. It presupposes and requires the attainment of critical maturity by the thinker or teacher who undertakes it. Naïve or partial attempts at dialectical appropriation only compound the problems they seek to address. But how does a finite individual distinguish the genuine and enduring from the inauthentic and transient in the great philosophical and cultural traditions of the past? The relevant philosophical criterion I have argued (*The Crisis of Philosophy, Authenticity as Self-Transcendence*) is the test of performative consistency.[31] Authentic philosophical positions invite development when they are intelligently understood and reasonably affirmed. The rival counter-positions, by contrast, invite reversal because at some level, tacit or explicit, they ignore or deny the conditions of their own possibility.

Moral, political, religious, and cultural traditions should be appraised by appealing to their sources and their outcomes. At the root of all authentic development are the *eros and exigence* of the human spirit. By the *eros* of the spirit, I mean the native human desire to understand what is experienced but not yet understood; to understand what is carefully attended to; to affirm what is true, negate what is false, and to suspend judgment when the available evidence is insufficient; to promote and preserve what is genuinely good, and to avoid and correct through reform what is not. By the *exigence* of the spirit, I mean the intrinsic norms governing the exercise of human subjectivity. These norms can be briefly articulated in four universal precepts: be attentive to the full range of experience; be intelligent in all instances of questioning and answering; be reasonable in reflecting, appraising the evidence and judging; be responsible in deliberating, deciding, acting, and ultimately remembering. The faithful observance of these principles and precepts, by individuals and communities, promotes excellence and justice throughout human life.[32]

But the high ideal of sustained faithful observance sets a standard from which actual practice regularly diverges. Fidelity to the precepts of the human spirit is repeatedly compromised by the manifold forms of bias or violence that obstruct authentic performance. Actual human living is the result of a complex interplay between the acceptance and refusal of self-transcendence. Our lifelong quest for understanding, our acknowledgement of the real, our pursuit of the good are constantly frustrated by inattention, bias, and excessive self-love. In one sense, the masters of suspicion are right; we are all disposed to conceal or mask these sources of personal and collective disorder, or to *rationalize* them away. Yet, our different strategies of concealment cannot escape the eventual verdict of history. The fruit of human authenticity, of sustained self-transcendence, is enduring development, reciprocal cooperation, and collaborative mutual influence. The fruits of bias, in their different forms, are isolation, breakdown, violence, and decline. In critically evaluating a cultural tradition, we are not limited to an appraisal of its intentional origins. Ultimately, it is by the character of their enduring fruits that we know and assess them.[33]

With these reflective criteria in mind, let me suggest five ways of encountering the past that exemplify the spirit of critical belonging for which I have called.

1. In the ancient world, Aristotle regularly began his reflections on a topic of inquiry with a critical review of the opinions of his predecessors. His interpretive assumption was that insight and oversight both belonged to the uneven inheritance of the past. On Aristotle's view, truth is a complex but unified whole, and our predecessors tend to reveal some limited part of it. As a general rule, they tend to be right in what they affirm and wrong in what they exclude or omit. Either way, whether they hit or miss the mark, they challenge us to get to the root of the matter ourselves.[34]

2. In the thirteenth century, Thomas Aquinas established an impressive model for appropriating an inherited set of conflicting traditions. His task was momentous: to bring into some measure of ordered unity the theological insights and oversights of four distinct cultures: the biblical culture of the ancient Jews, the philosophical culture of the classical Greeks, the theological culture of the Christian patristics, and the Islamic culture of the great Arab commentators on Aristotle. His *Summa Theologiae* is an integrative masterpiece that stands as an enduring example of what critical appropriation can achieve in an historical context of intense multi-culturalism.[35]

3. In recent years, Alasdair MacIntyre and Bernard Lonergan have shown how the complex intellectual tradition to which Aristotle and Aquinas

belong can be transformed in the light of historical consciousness. MacIntyre's *After Virtue* and Lonergan's *Verbum* and *Insight* constitute notable attempts to preserve the insights and remedy the limitations of the enduring Aristotelean tradition in ethics, cognitional theory, and metaphysics.[36]

4. In explicit contrast to post-modern genealogies of suspicion, contemporary *narratives of critical retrieval* seek to recover what has been lost or suppressed by modern unmasking and forgetfulness. They seek to explain or redress the strong modern temptation to deny or remain silent about the depth of our moral and political commitments. Good examples of this interpretive model include: Robert Bellah's *Habits of the Heart*; Hannah Arendt's effort in *Between Past and Future* and *On Revolution* to retrieve the republican tradition of civic humanism; and Charles Taylor's *Sources of the Self* and *A Secular Age,* which carefully articulate and thus help to retrieve the full range of constitutive goods and moral sources on which our modern identity actually depends.

5. Finally, there is the remarkable interpretive project of Paul Ricoeur, which recognizes both the tension and potential complementarity between the *hermeneutics of retrieval* and the *hermeneutics of suspicion.* Ricoeur openly acknowledges the historical importance of the critique of ideology and false consciousness. Appeals to tradition, authority, and ancestral custom continue to be used in defense of unjustifiable beliefs, practices, and institutions. There is no human principle, however sound in itself, that is not subject to misuse and distortion. But the hermeneutics of suspicion is blind if it bases its critique of the present on a wholesale emancipation of the past. All meaningful critique draws on one part of our cultural inheritance to oppose the limitations of another. As Ricoeur wisely and ironically reminds us, the French Revolutionary ideal of deliverance from the bondage of the *Ancien Regime* is actually rooted in the central episodes of our biblical traditions, the Exodus of the Jews from bondage in Egypt, and Jesus' deliverance from death through the resurrection.[37]

The practice of critical appropriation then is a deliberate attempt to bridge the divide between the hermeneutics of retrieval and the hermeneutics of suspicion. Both of these interpretive orientations are legitimate, for every cultural tradition contains elements that are worthy of retrieval and others that are unfit for transmission. Still, it is important to be critical about the posture of criticism itself. Hermeneutic suspicion is an ambiguous interpretive outlook, even though it has become the dominant critical stance in contemporary academic culture. We too often grant allegiance to traditions that are inauthentic and ideological, but we also, as Taylor and Polanyi have

shown, espouse alienation from much that is genuine and good.[38] The evaluative interpretation and appraisal of a tradition is conditioned by the personal
horizon and authenticity of the interpreter. But that horizon is as subject to
inauthenticity as the traditions against which it is directed. In assessing a radical critic like Nietzsche, Foucault, or Rorty, it is always essential to ask: how
balanced and accurate are the genealogical narratives they create as weapons
of criticism; how coherent and credible are the critical principles underlying
their deconstructive activity?

I am in full accord with this timely judgment of Ricoeur: "Nothing is more
necessary today than to renounce the *arrogance of critique* and to carry out
with patience and humility the endless work of distancing and renewing our
historical substance."[39] Patience, tenacity, cooperation, and humility will all
be needed to see us through the modern predicament. The example of our
celebrated antecedents, like Descartes, is sobering, for these qualities were
notably lacking at the inception of modernity. Will late modernity simply
repeat the extravagance of its origin? It clearly does not have to. And for the
sake of our students, ourselves and our world, let us hope it does not.

At this time, our greatest need is for a critical center of collaborating
thinkers who are able to understand, appreciate, and responsibly criticize
both the old and the new.[40] Their ample and generous vision is necessary if
we are to overcome the deceptive antinomy all of us were bequeathed by the
contentious quarrel between the ancients and the moderns. As the victorious
moderns interpreted that quarrel, they saw it as a conflict between the ancient
commitment to the authority of the past and their own passionate dedica-
tion to the promise of the future. But this alleged antinomy is divisive and
misleading, as the great French thinker, Alexis de Tocqueville so well understood. Allow me to close these reflections with a quotation of de Tocqueville,
and let it stand as the intended moral of this essay and this book. "It is our
common concern for the future that drives our thought back into the past,
even to the remotest antiquity [. . .]For when the past ceases to cast its light
on the future, then the human mind wanders in obscurity."[41]

What our students, what our contemporaries, what our democracies des-
perately need at this time is less obscurity and more light. Let us humbly and
gratefully accept the light from whatever source it comes and transmit it to
others as faithfully and reliably as we can. That is our true calling as teachers
and citizens.

NOTES

1. Hannah Arendt, *Between Past and Future* (New York: Viking, 1969) 173–96.
"Education is the point at which we decide whether we love the world enough and by

the same token save it from that ruin which, except for renewal, except for the coming of the new and young would be inevitable." 196.

2. My understanding of Modernity is deeply indebted to the thought of Charles Taylor, particularly to the critical retrieval he achieves in *Sources of the Self* (Cambridge: Harvard University Press, 1989).

3. Aristotle *De Anima* 403 b 22.

4. See Michael Polanyi, *Personal Knowledge* (Chicago: Chicago University Press, 1962) and Charles Taylor, *The Ethics of Authenticity* (Cambridge: Harvard University Press, 1991) and *Philosophy and the Human Sciences* (Cambridge: Cambridge University Press, 1985).

5. "This thing about which we are most serious, the point of view which constitutes our enlightenment and our emancipation, will appear in coming ages to have been our myth." John Dunne, *The City of the Gods: A Study in Myth and Mortality* (New York; Macmillan, 1965) v.

6. Saul Bellow, *Herzog* (New York: Penguin, 1996) 56. The theme is recurrent in Bellow's novels, especially *Mr. Sammler's Planet* (New York: Penguin, 1995).

7. "It is characteristic of the intellectual life of our culture that it fosters a form of assent which does not involve actual credence . . . many among us find it gratifying to entertain the thought that alienation is to be overcome only by the completeness of alienation, and that alienation completed is not a deprivation but a potency." Lionel Trilling, *Sincerity and Authenticity* (Cambridge: Harvard University Press, 1972) 171.

8. "We tend in our culture to stifle the spirit. . . . We have read so many goods out of our official story, we have buried their power so deep beneath layers of philosophical rationale, that they are in danger of stifling. Or rather, since they are our goods, human goods, we are stifling." (Taylor, *Sources of the Self*) 520.

9. At the core of our pre-modern inheritance are the cultural traditions of Athens, Rome and Jerusalem. At the center of Modernity are the scientific revolution of the seventeenth century and the radical expansion of historical consciousness in the nineteenth. At the heart of the post-modern, as I understand it, is the heuristic shift from identity to difference and the hermeneutic privileging of the traditionally marginal.

10. See Hannah Arendt, *The Human Condition* (Chicago: University of Chicago Press, 1958) 7–21.

11. Alexis de Tocqueville, *Democracy in America* (New York: Doubleday Anchor, 1969) 287. See also, Robert Bellah et al, *Habits of the Heart* (New York: Harper, 1985).

12. Polanyi, *Personal Knowledge*, 203–45.

13. Aristotle, *Nicomachean Ethics* 1103 a 33. *The Basic Works of Aristotle* (New York: Random House, 1941) 952.

14. "We must now recognize belief once more as the source of all knowledge. Tacit assent and intellectual passions, the sharing of an idiom and of a cultural heritage, affiliation to a like-minded community: such are the impulses which shape our vision of the nature of things. No intelligence, however critical or original, can operate outside such a fiduciary framework." Michael Polanyi, *Personal Knowledge*, 266. For the role of belief in scientific inquiry, see Bernard Lonergan's "Belief: Today's Issue," *A Second Collection* (Philadelphia: Westminster Press, 1974) 87–99. "The difference

between common sense and scientific knowledge is not a different proportion of belief, but a more effective control of belief." Lonergan, A Second *Collection*, 88.

15. Hans Georg Gadamer, *Truth and Method* (London: Sheed and Ward, 1975).

16. Polanyi, *Personal Knowledge*, 212–37.

17. See Charles Taylor, "The Ethics of Inarticulacy," *Sources of the Self*, 53–90.

18. See Hannah Arendt, "What Is Authority?" *Between Past and Future*, 119–41.

19. "To accept nothing as true which I did not clearly recognize to be so. That is to say, carefully to avoid precipitation and prejudice in judgments, and to accept in them nothing more than was presented to my mind so clearly and distinctly that I could have no occasion to doubt it." Rene Descartes, *Discourse on Method, Part II, The Philosophical Works of Descartes* (New York: Cambridge University Press, 1970) I, 92.

20. See Michael Polanyi, "The Critique of Doubt," *Personal Knowledge*, 269–98. "The developing power of disengaged self-responsible reason has tended to accredit a view of the subject as an unsituated, even punctual self . . . much of the most insightful philosophy of the twentieth century has gone to refute this picture of the disengaged subject." (Taylor, *Sources of the Self*, 514).

21. See Sigmund Freud, *Introductory Lectures on Psychoanalysis* (London: Hogarth, 1963) 285 and "A Philosophy of Life," *New Introductory Lectures on Psychoanalysis* (New York: Norton, 1933) 216–49.

22. For Freud's critique of the utopian strain in Marxism, see "A Philosophy of Life," *New Introductory Lectures on Psychanalysis*. According to Lionel Trilling, Freud stands "like a lion in the path of all hopes of achieving happiness through the radical revision of social life." (*Sincerity and Authenticity*, 151).

23. See Paul Ricoeur, *Freud and Philosophy: An Essay in Interpretation* (New Haven: Yale University Press, 1970).

24. See Alasdair MacIntyre, *Three Rival Versions of Moral Inquiry* (Notre Dame: University of Notre Dame Press, 1990) 32–55. As Marx uses the term "ideology" it refers to a cultural justification of an exploitative economic order. My own use of "ideology" as a term of criticism derives from Bernard Lonergan. "A man is his true self inasmuch as he is self-transcending. Inversely, a man is alienated from his true self inasmuch as he refuses self-transcendence, and the basic form of ideology is the self-justification of alienated man." Lonergan, *Method in Theology* (New York: Herder and Herder, 1972) 337.

25. MacIntyre, *Three Versions of Moral Inquiry*, 35.

26. For the concept of moral inversion, see Michael Polanyi, *Personal Knowledge*, 226–37.

27. See Charles Taylor, "Foucault on Freedom and Truth," *Philosophy and the Human Sciences* (New York: Cambridge University Press, 1985) 152–84.

28. "What sort of freak then is man! How novel, how monstrous, how chaotic, how paradoxical, how prodigious! Judge of all things, feeble earth worm, repository of truth, sink of doubt and error, glory and refuse of the universe! Who will unravel such a tangle?" Blaise Pascal, *Pensées* (New York: Penguin, 1965) #64.

29. "We truly shy away from any systematic discussion of human strength . . . we do our tortured best to express what we value in in terms of double negatives: a person

whom we would declare reasonably well is relatively resistant to aggression, or somewhat freer from repression, or less given to ambivalence than might be expected." Erik Erikson, *Insight and Responsibility* (New York: Norton, 1964) 112.

30. It is important to acknowledge two aspects of the postmodern enterprise. The hermeneutics of suspicion is rigorously applied to the dominant traditions of the West, while hermeneutic sympathy and understanding are extended to marginalized cultures and peoples. Telling the stories of the past from the other side is a belated form of narrative justice. It has yielded critical insights and needed correctives to the prejudices of those formerly or presently in power. These needed contributions to hermeneutic justice are deeply welcome. My critical reservations about postmodernism are based on the one-sidedness of the hermeneutics of suspicion.

31. See Michael McCarthy, *The Crisis of Philosophy* (Albany: State University of New York Press, 1990) 295–318. And "Pluralism, Invariance and Conflict," *The Review of Metaphysics* 51 (September 1997) 3–23.

32. This compressed account of the eros and exigence of the human spirit is based on the detailed analysis of intentional subjectivity developed by Bernard Lonergan. For a fuller presentation of Lonergan's analysis, see *Insight: A Study of Human Understanding* (New York: Philosophical Library, 1970).

33. The credibility of this appraisal is no less dependent on the authenticity of the critics who make it. "Not only can some potentially destructive ideals be directed to genuine goods: some of them undoubtedly are. The ethic of Plato and the Stoics can't be written off as mere illusion. And even non-believers, if they don't block it off, will feel a powerful appeal in the gospel, which they will interpret in a secular fashion, just as Christians, unless immured in unblinkered self-sufficiency, will recognize the appalling destruction wrought in history in the name of faith." It is, however, facile criticism to take these self-destructive consequences as a refutation of its validity. This makes "what I believe is the cardinal mistake of believing that a good must be invalid if it leads to suffering or destruction." Taylor, *Sources of the Self*, 519–20.

34. Aristotle, *Metaphysics* 993b: *The Basic Works of Aristotle*, 712.

35. See Alasdair MacIntyre, "Aquinas and the Rationality of Tradition," *Three Rival Versions of Moral Inquiry*, 127–48.

36. See MacIntyre, "Aristotle's Account of the Virtues," *After Virtue*, 146–64. See also Lonergan, "Aquinas Today: Tradition and Innovation" *A Third Collection* (Mahwah: Paulist Press, 1985) 35–54.

37. See Paul Ricoeur, *Political and Social Essays* (Athens: University of Ohio Press, 1974) and *Hermeneutics and the Human Sciences* (Cambridge: Cambridge University Press, 1981).

38. In this essay, authenticity requires sustained fidelity to the eros and exigence of the human spirit. Alienation, inauthenticity, results when those requirements are not met due to bias in its multiple forms. Ideology is the justification of alienation, of the refusal or failure to meet the high demands of personal or communal self-transcendence.

39. I believe this quote comes from *Hermeneutics and the Human Sciences*, but I have been unable to find its location in the text.

40. Bernard Lonergan, *Collection* (Toronto: Toronto University Press, 1988) 266–67.

41. Alexis de Tocqueville, *Democracy in America*, Volume II (New York: Vintage, 1945) 349.

Chapter 6

Democracy in America

The Sources of Our Discontent

"Men will not receive the truth from their enemies; and it is very seldom offered to them by their friends."

Alexis de Tocqueville, *Democracy in America*, Volume II

In 1831, a young aristocratic Frenchman, Alexis de Tocqueville, and his friend Gustave Beaumont received permission from the French government to study the penal system of the United States. They arrived in New York City on May 11, 1831, and returned to France nine months later on February 20, 1832. At the time of his visit, Tocqueville was twenty-six years old.

During his stay in America, Tocqueville travelled from Boston in the east to Green Bay in the west; from Sault Ste Marie in the north to New Orleans in the south, a total of over 7,000 miles. He closely observed American customs and habits, interviewed both ordinary and distinguished citizens, did historical research in local and national records, kept a personal diary, and reflected on the sources of American liberty, as well as the dangers threatening liberty in a democratic age.

To put Tocqueville's famous journey into context, it had been 211 years since the Pilgrims landed at Plymouth, 56 years since the revolutionary skirmishes at Lexington and Concord, 45 years since the adoption of the Federal Constitution; and it would be another 30 years before the outbreak of the Civil War and the founding of Vassar College. When Tocqueville arrived in New York, the United States had just entered a new political era, the age of Jacksonian democracy. Andrew Jackson was the first westerner to be elected president. His administration coincided with the extension of the electoral franchise, an increase in democratic populism, a marked expansion in presidential power, the candid acceptance of the spoils system in politics (to the

electoral victor and his allies belong the spoils of government), and a markedly lower level of political leadership than had existed during the Revolution
and the first four decades of the American presidency.

Two years after Tocqueville and Beaumont returned to France, they published a report on the American penal system and its practical relevance
for French prison reform. This report, the ostensible purpose of their visit
to America, is primarily of scholarly interest today. But the more enduring fruit of Tocqueville's American travels were his two-volume study of
Democracy in America, with the first volume published in 1835 and the second in 1840. Volume I concentrates on the political effects of democracy as
a principle of social organization; Volume II examines the cultural effects of
democracy, its discernible influence on the intellectual, moral, and spiritual
constitution of American society.

Tocqueville himself was born into a dying world as a new one struggled
to be born. His birth coincided with the violent destruction of the aristocratic French feudal order, the *Ancien Regime*, and his life overlapped with
the great democratic revolutions in North America and Europe. The central
theme of *Democracy in America* was the uncertain fate of liberty in these
new democratic societies. Tocqueville supported the emerging democracies
because they were more just than their aristocratic predecessors. "A state of
democratic equality is perhaps less elevated than aristocratic hierarchy, but it
is more just, and it is the justice of democracy that constitutes its greatness
and beauty" (*Democracy in America*, Vol II, 349–352). At the same time, he
was troubled by the dangers a democratic society and government posed to
liberty and to an elevated conception of the human being.[1]

What are the dangers to liberty in the "irreversible" movement of modern history toward democratic equality? According to Tocqueville, liberty
is threatened by the following constellation of forces: a dramatic growth in
the power of the central government, which becomes increasingly remote,
bureaucratic, and paternalistic; the loss of intermediate political associations that moderate the relations between democratic citizens and the central
authority;[2] a retreat by democratic individuals into the narrow confines of
their private lives with a corresponding disengagement from public affairs.
Tocqueville describes this troubling political phenomenon as "democratic
individualism."[3] When these factors coalesce, the probable result, he
believed, is a new form of despotism, the despotism of the democratic majority, in which the isolated individual is left powerless before the bureaucratic
state and the tyranny of majority opinion.

In brilliant and memorable prose, Tocqueville explains why democratic
despotism is especially to be dreaded by the friends of liberty.[4] It makes
the life and property of human beings insecure; it weakens their civil and
individual rights, like the right to free speech and freedom of worship; and

as despotism has traditionally done, it abolishes meaningful political liberty, the effective participation of ordinary citizens in the regular practice of self-government. Based on his experiences and conversations in America, Tocqueville concluded that the despotism of the democratic majority was a permanent threat, not an historical inevitability. After observing public life in the New England townships, he argued that preserving local political liberty was the strongest protection against the majoritarian tyranny he feared.[5] Adopting Montesquieu's concept of free republican government, he modified its definition to fit the circumstances of continental republics, like the United States, in democratic age.[6] And he outlined a new science of republican politics based on the following principles: the decentralizing of public administration; the distribution of political power toward local units of authority (the principle of subsidiarity); the reliance on voluntary associations to mediate the transactions between citizens and their government; the genuinely enlightened self-interest of a democratic people firmly committed to the rule of law, a free and independent judiciary and press, and the educated readiness of citizens to participate responsibly in public life. For Tocqueville, an active, informed, responsible citizenry was the best, perhaps the only, antidote to the poison of democratic individualism. "Feelings and opinions are recruited, the heart is enlarged, and the mind developed by the reciprocal influence of human beings on one another" (Vol II, 117).[7]

Though *Democracy in America* was written nearly two-hundred years ago, it remains, in my judgment, the single greatest study of the American character that we possess. But time, of course, does not stand still. So, what do we find when we revisit American democracy today, not as foreign travelers, but as deeply concerned citizens. One of the clearest and most penetrating accounts of the existing political situation in the United States is offered by William Galston of the Brookings Institution.[8]

Galston believes that our present political crisis has arisen because a transformative period in American public life has come to an end. This impressive period of political creativity is closely associated with the presidencies of two Roosevelts, Theodore, and Franklin. The closing decades of the nineteenth century and the opening decades of the twentieth were marked by progressive political thinking in the United States.

In the gilded age context of unregulated capitalism and the monopoly of economic and political power by industrial interests (a threat Tocqueville hadn't really foreseen), critical economic reforms, including anti-trust and labor legislation and the graduated income tax, as well as the beginning of national environmental policy were enacted during the presidencies of Theodore Roosevelt and Woodrow Wilson. Franklin Roosevelt's New Deal, during the Great Depression, and Lyndon Johnson's Great Society initiatives during the economic boom of the 1960s dramatically expanded these earlier

progressive policies. Most of the environmental and social welfare legislation of the United States (social security, unemployment insurance, aid to
dependent children, worker's compensation, Medicare, Medicaid, and the
creation of the federal regulatory agencies) derive from this sixty-year period
of political activism and pragmatic social reform.

The progressive tide began to turn, however, in the 1960s when the
struggle for civil rights and the divisiveness of the Vietnam War destroyed
Roosevelt's New Deal coalition. In 1964, the Republican party nominated
Barry Goldwater, an outspoken political conservative, as their candidate
for president. Johnson's crushing defeat of Goldwater provided the political
impetus for passing the historic civil rights bills of the mid-nineteen sixties,
but it also cost the Democrats their electoral control over the solid south.[9] In
a reversal of dramatic proportions, the Republicans replaced the Democrats
as the majority party in the southern United States. This critical shift in partisan allegiance played a major role in the Republicans' electoral successes in
presidential, congressional, and state legislative campaigns after 1968.

The national movement for civil rights, both for racial minorities and
women, the demoralizing defeat in Vietnam, the counter-cultural excesses of
the sixties and seventies, the weakening of the American labor movement,
the demographic shift to the sunbelt, and the oil shocks and hyper-inflation
of the 1970s effectively converged to end the great progressive era of the
New Deal.[10] One of Goldwater's ardent supporters, Ronald Reagan, won
two presidential terms by appealing to wounded national pride, consolidat-
ing Southern and evangelical support, and by escalating the conservative
critique of the federal government's legislative and regulatory agenda. Using
the glib jargon of modern advertising, Reagan argued that the federal government is the major source of our national problems, rather than an essential
participant in addressing effectively our common and unmet needs. Reagan
promoted a new conservative orthodoxy that was radically anti-government
and pro-market in its public rhetoric and mindset. In principle, he rejected the
mixed economy of the New Deal, though in practice he was unable to reverse
the growth of most federal programs. Still, Reagan's neo-conservative agenda
clearly moved the country to the right politically and culturally, and put the
proponents of social, economic, and environmental justice on the defensive.[11]

The bitter political stalemate in Washington since the Reagan era has been
between those who seek to preserve and develop the progressive legacy of the
New Deal (the clear majority within the national Democratic party) and those
who seek to weaken or abolish the core elements of America's moderate welfare state (the conservative majority among the Republicans, now augmented
by the populist passions of the Tea Party and Trump's "Make America Great
Again" loyalists).[12]

Stepping back from the bitter partisan passions of the moment, I want to explore three powerful sources of discontent within American democracy today: economic anxiety, cultural fragmentation (the loss of a cohesive civic community), and the decline of public confidence in our major democratic institutions.[13]

Contemporary economic anxiety has three related aspects: economic inequality, economic insecurity, and the concentration of economic power. At the root of national economic anxiety is an historic transformation in the American economy. The United States is structurally changing from an industrial mass production economy, based heavily on unskilled labor, to a global information economy based on continuous technological innovation, the global movement of capital, technical knowledge and jobs, and the constant need to upgrade skills for an unstable and highly competitive labor market. The dynamic technological revolution, the competitive challenges of globalization, heightened sensitivity to the environmental dangers of unregulated growth, and the marked decline in needed public investment and support have created a nest of difficult, often intractable, problems for democratic policy makers, planners, and citizens.[14]

INEQUALITY

During the post-war boom (1945–1972), which Eric Hobsbawm has called the golden age of capitalism, the fruits of American prosperity were broadly shared. The rising tide of the mixed economy lifted all boats, as inequalities of wealth and income measurably diminished. A greatly improved standard of living, based on sustained economic growth, full employment, and rising productivity became widely available to the American middle class.

During the last five decades, however, since the oil shocks of 1973, the greater competitiveness of the global market, and numerous failures in public economic policy, the annual incomes of the majority of American citizens stagnated or fell, while the dramatic gains in wealth were enjoyed by a very small minority. As America again became a more class-stratified society, the post-war political consensus collapsed, causing a troubling decline in civic solidarity within the nation as a whole. Those at the peak of the economic pyramid prospered as never before, while the middle class, despite the massive entry of women into the labor force, became financially squeezed and discouraged. With growing conservative opposition to an activist government and the radical restructuring of the economy, the poor and unskilled fell even further behind.[15]

A new underclass emerged in the nation's cities whose economic and social plight has largely remained unaddressed. The most troubling dynamic was that economic and social inequalities regularly translated into massive disparities in educational achievement. In the new global economy, these disparities of competence led to limited economic opportunities, often crippling social pathologies, and political withdrawal and disaffection among the very citizens most in need of public support. While the condition of the elderly improved, due to highly effective political organization, the inner city and rural poor lost even more ground. Even worse, they lost an effective and reliable political constituency actively committed to social and economic justice for the least advantaged Americans.[16]

INSECURITY

The global information society shatters the traditional expectations of American workers. In the older industrial economy, workers could often expect to have one employer and one career for the whole of their working life. There were periods of cyclical unemployment corresponding to declines in the business cycle, but the combined efforts of business, government, organized labor, and supportive local communities provided the great majority of workers with a measure of economic security.

In the new global economy, that security has largely disappeared. Automation results in a permanent loss of manufacturing jobs. Repeated "downsizing," constant mergers and acquisitions, disruptive plant closings, the pressure of international competition, and the lack of employer loyalty have both blue-collar and white-collar workers understandably anxious about the future. As the power of organized labor has declined, employers seek regularly to reduce the benefits they offer, often resorting to temporary and part-time contractual relations without any benefits at all.[17] High levels of economic insecurity threaten individual workers, their families and neighborhoods, and whole regions of the country like the rust belts of the north and Midwest. The new international division of labor has meant structural as well as cyclical unemployment, and a major shift in the balance of power between capital and labor. This dangerous imbalance has been magnified under Republican governments ideologically committed to market fundamentalism and financially dependent on great corporate and financial wealth.[18]

POWER

The third source of anxiety is concentrated and unchecked economic power. Because of globalization, individual nations and governments have lost a substantial measure of control over their economic destinies. Multi-national corporations often operate beyond the effective reach of fiscal and regulatory power. But the deeper sources of change include technological innovation and diffusion, the unregulated flow of capital and investment, and a highly competitive global market in labor, information, goods, and services. These momentous changes have further weakened existing political authorities, while allowing concentrated economic power to grow unchecked.[19]

We find ourselves, sadly, in a political situation analogous to that of the late nineteenth century. At that time, responding to the leadership of progressive reformers, national governments began to assert their authority over the unregulated power of the trusts. Government ceased to be the protective ally of the powerful and became a dedicated voice for the weak and disadvantaged. This shift in political priorities was later consolidated under the New Deal and the Great Society. The eventual collapse of the New Deal coalition, however, meant the end of the national progressive consensus and the corresponding rise in economic inequality and political injustice.

Our three sources of economic anxiety are interdependent. Inequalities of wealth, power, and political influence are mutually reinforcing. Powerful interest groups use money, lobbyists, and organizational resources to influence government officials who then shape public policies and rules that disproportionately advantage the already well off. The benefits and burdens of national life are unfairly distributed. Recognizing these systemic inequalities, but uncertain how to correct them, large numbers of citizens become disaffected and withdraw from the political struggle, or seek scapegoats for their problems among immigrants and racial, religious, and ethnic minorities.[20] Even though sustained, informed, and responsible political engagement is needed to reverse their economic and political decline, pervasive alienation from "politics as usual" either prevents the majority from collaborating on their own behalf, or makes them susceptible to self-serving demagogues like Trump and his "populist allies." In this way, a vicious cycle is created that perpetuates systemic injustice, threatens democratic norms and institutions, and deepens public discontent and division.[21]

THE DECLINE OF CIVIL SOCIETY

A second important source of democratic unrest is the decline in America's civil society.[22] The term "civil society" refers to the broad range of voluntary institutions and public associations that mediate between individual citizens on the one hand and governmental agencies and the competitive marketplace on the other. A healthy and unified democracy requires a strong and effective civil society because representative government on a national scale is often remote, impersonal, and bureaucratic, while economic markets are mercilessly driven by a zeal for maximizing profit. Since the major participants in global markets are often more remote and less accountable than government officials, the political activities of civil society are especially important today.

Tocqueville credited civil society, which he called "independent secondary powers" with three major contributions to democratic liberty.[23] They check concentrations of political and economic power; they help to secure and extend individual rights; and they provide essential public forums for civic education, where ordinary citizens learn the arts of cooperative action and the effective expression of political dissent. As independent centers of democratic power, they serve to counteract the hegemonic or despotic tendencies of both centralized government and the market economy.

Important examples of these intermediary powers include strong and influential families, neighborhood associations, churches, schools, colleges and universities, a free, independent, and responsible press, political parties, labor unions, charitable foundations, a complex array of voluntary associations, political, religious, moral, intellectual, cultural, ecological, and economic.[24]

These intermediate associations play an indispensable role in creating an informed, engaged, and responsible democratic citizenry. Their communal spirit checks the democratic tendency to narrow self-interest and the democratic passions for material prosperity and comfort. They provide critical arenas of social trust and cooperative action where citizens learn to accommodate differences of interest, opinion, and judgment. It is within civil society that ordinary men and women become responsible citizens, that they learn to know, love, and act on behalf of the whole community. Not only do these "grammar schools of liberty" cultivate the arts and virtues of citizenship, drawing individuals out of their private homes and interests and into the public realm, but they also create common sites for pursuing important human goods that are neither political nor economic in nature: familial love, reciprocal friendship, disinterested knowledge, the performance and enjoyment of the arts, religious worship, the free exchange of ideas and opinions on every topic of human concern.[25]

Galston agrees with Robert Putnam and Charles Taylor that American civil society, and therefore the principal sources of American civic education, are showing serious signs of erosion and decay: families are weaker and the marital bond more fragile; neighborhoods are less cohesive and therefore less secure; our schools provide deeply unequal educations for our children; the university's moral and civic authority has markedly declined; the public media have become increasingly shrill, superficial, and profit driven; labor unions, churches, political parties, traditional civic associations are declining in membership and influence. What Tocqueville called the vice of "democratic individualism" is becoming widespread. "Private life in democratic times is so busy, so excited, so filled with wishes and work that hardly any energy or leisure remains to each individual for public life."[26]

As the intermediate institutions of civil society weaken, democratic citizens tend to feel isolated from and indifferent to the larger society. The focus of their attention turns inward. They live within the important but narrow circle of self, family, and friends; they mistakenly think and act as though their private destinies were disconnected from those of their fellow citizens and the rest of humanity. Isolated citizens, discontent with their plight, while lacking reliable knowledge of worldly realities, injustices, dangers, and concentrations of power are easily manipulated by propaganda, scapegoating, deliberate lies, and distorted media coverage. When their interest is drawn to politics, it is personal scandal, collective scapegoating, and orchestrated campaigns of resentment that normally capture their attention and concern. American politics, since the extreme partisanship of Newt Gingrich, the rise of the Tea Party, and the unbridled demagoguery of Donald Trump and his media allies clearly illustrates this divisive pattern.[27]

THE EROSION OF POLITICAL AUTHORITY

In the founders' vision of democracy, politics, the symbol of the commonweal, enjoyed directive authority over economics, the symbol of self-interested activity. Today, American politics is heavily dominated by economic interests and market-oriented models.[28] The conduct of government increasingly resembles economic activity as bargaining, public relations, and partisan advocacy become pervasive. Nearly everyone conceives of politics as a way of advancing private and limited group concerns. Periodic references to the common good or the general welfare become largely ceremonial and vacuous. These normative democratic ideals bear almost no relation to what is really going on.

In this cynical atmosphere, the wealthiest and best organized economic interests gain even greater influence on government. Economic power readily translates into political power. Public officials become heavily dependent on wealthy individuals, business corporations, labor unions, and political action committees to defray the staggering costs of their electoral campaigns. (a grave problem only compounded by the Supreme Court's one-sided ruling in *Citizens United*).[29] Lobbyists, the professional advocates for well-organized interest groups, have become the critical intermediary figures in American politics, devising electoral strategies, soliciting contributions, and shaping or opposing public policy and legislation. Concentrated corporate wealth and special interests of every kind employ lobbyists, lawyers, public relations and media experts, even hired intellectuals and ideologically based think tanks, to advance their political agenda. There is no shortage of political activity or discourse, but they are almost exclusively self-interested and partisan.

The loss of governmental independence, impartiality, and effectiveness has caused a steady erosion in the substance of our democratic faith. Most Americans now believe that the people are governed by their elected representatives for the benefit of an influential and selfish minority.[30] (For Tocqueville the great threat to democratic liberty was the despotism of the majority; for us it has become the tyranny of well-organized and self-serving minorities). While professional lobbyists actively promote the economic advantage of their clients, partisan pleading is not restricted to business and labor. The gun lobby, the religious right, and various pressure groups on the political left exercise political influence wholly disproportionate to their electoral strength.

The troubling conviction that our government serves the interests of the powerful and well organized has had a demoralizing effect on American democracy. It has dramatically weakened public confidence in government, generated contempt for public officials and institutions, and significantly reduced the political engagement of ordinary citizens. The signs of political alienation are everywhere: declining levels of voter participation; reduced attention to and knowledge of world affairs; the political indifference, impatience, and disaffection of the young; the reluctance of serious public spirited citizens to enter political life; the restriction of public debate to the formulaic chatter of journalists and entertainers; the disproportionate influence of sensationalist media and deliberate propaganda in shaping political perceptions and judgments; the absence of honest, informed, and justice-centered discussions about taxes, regulations, public policies, and government services; the immediate resort to litigation as a remedy for perceived injustice; the deepening sense of political impotence and despair (we no longer think and act as a unified people to meet our fiduciary obligations to posterity).[31]

Public cynicism about politics and the pervasive distrust of government are harmful to American democracy. They strengthen the vice of democratic individualism, lessen effective and responsible civic participation, increase the influence of the wealthy, the powerful, and the demagogic, and diminish the prospects for significant economic and political reform. Nearly 250 years after the creation of the United States, the great American experiment in democratic self-government is in serious trouble.[32]

GENUINE DEMOCRATIC REFORM

The most powerful forces at work in our culture are anti-political. Their dominance of the public sphere helps to account for the erosion of political authority and the sad state of civic engagement and trust. Four challenges

seem particularly urgent for American democracy today: the political challenge of globalization; the need to articulate a new and credible federalism;
the recreation of a vibrant, generous, and non-partisan civic community; and
the deliberate spread of disinformation and lies for narrow partisan ends.

The integration of the global economy and the competitiveness of the
global market require democratic theorists to rethink the relationship between
economic and political power. Many of the political institutions shaped by
modernity have been subverted by global capitalism. Most national governments can no longer control the economic well-being of their countries. In
a troubling repetition of the "gilded age," democratic politics has lost its
effective authority over economics. If we are to create appropriate political
institutions for the global economy, we will need new forms of democratic
authority, new structures of international law, and new patterns of transna-
tional cooperation capable of regulating global finance and commerce without stifling its prosperity creating potential. We will need to develop through
flexible experimentation an international analogue of the mixed economy
that emerged during the progressive era. The mixed economy combines free
enterprise and commerce with state regulation and oversight, while making
collective provision for essential public goods and recurrent social needs.
As Charles Taylor has argued, mixed economies seek to create an effective
interactive balance between political and economic requirements that tend to
undercut each other.[33]

Toward a Global Federalism

The federal principle of government recognizes the complementarity of multiple centers of political power. These centers of power in a global society
should begin at the local level and extend outwards to the county, the state,
and the nation, culminating in international centers of authority. To avoid
conflicting jurisdictions, a genuine federalism must respect the principle of
subsidiarity. Public responsibilities and obligations should be assigned to the
lowest level of authority capable of meeting their practical demands. The evident attractions of local control, however, do not obviate the need for a strong
and independent federal government and for carefully designed global institutions. But what is the proper balance today between local, state, national, and
international authorities and between the essential obligations of government
and the contributions of civil society?[34]

To answer these questions wisely, and without ideological bias, we need
contemporary thinkers with the realism and insight of the early American fed-
eralists. Political decentralization has the advantage of localizing power and
accountability and creating opportunities for independent civic initiatives.
Municipal institutions remain the strength of free nations, as Tocqueville

insisted. They bring government near the people and teach ordinary citizens the democratic arts of shared deliberation, constructive compromise, and responsible dissent. There remains, however, a continuing need for federal power to conduct foreign policy, to defend legitimate national interests, to oversee the economy, to protect the environment, to support the weak and the vulnerable, and to provide an effective counterweight to economic forces that local communities lack the power to resist or restrain.

While the need for institutional and cultural reform is evident, sobriety and realism are also required. Politics, at every level of engagement, is an uncertain enterprise. Human beings invariably bring their hopes and prejudices, their knowledge and ignorance, their selfishness and generosity into the public realm of action and speech. There are deeply important goods at stake in democratic politics, peace, justice, liberty, security, prosperity, and enhanced community, but the risk of political failure and demoralization is always high.[35]

E PLURIBUS UNUM: THE CHALLENGE
OF CONTEMPORARY PLURALISM

Revised immigration laws and shifting demographic patterns have transformed the American electorate during the last fifty years. With the dramatic increase in immigrants from Latin America, southeast Asia, the Pacific rim, and the Middle East has come a far more complex ethnic and racial consciousness. Traditional divisions between black and white have been partly blurred by intermarriage and by a new body politic composed of Nicaraguans, Koreans, Indians, Iranians, and Mexicans, to name only a few of our fellow Americans. New sources of political identity and loyalty have also emerged based on gender, religion, and sexual orientation. We can no longer speak, as Tocqueville serenely did, of the Anglo-Americans unified by their common religious and moral convictions.[36] Between Tocqueville's era and our own, new democratic realities have intervened, irreversibly changing the political culture of the United States: industrialization, urbanization, secularization, and globalization. Most Americans today are no longer farmers, and they no longer live in small towns and villages. While the great majority still believe in God, the biblically-based moral community that reassured Tocqueville in the 1830s has steadily declined. Tocqueville looked to Christianity and patriotism as unifying forces within American democracy. But the religious, ethnic, and moral pluralism of contemporary America undermines his articulated hopes for a unified national community rooted in common religious and cultural traditions.[37]

Earlier waves of immigration transformed America in the nineteenth century as well. Irish Catholics from the north, Italians from the south, Jews from the ghettos of central and eastern Europe flooded American cities and challenged the hegemony of the white Protestant majority. Those fierce tensions were eventually resolved by time, education, intermarriage, shared military service, and working-class solidarity. A new civil religion and a new internationalist patriotism emerged from World War II, as the great American melting pot blended its ethnically and religiously diverse citizens together. (African Americans and native Americans remained the scandalous exception to this integrative pattern).[38] The liberation movements of the sixties and seventies, demanding civil rights for everyone, equal treatment of women, full respect for every ethnic group, and the public acceptance of gays and lesbians have shattered the melting pot imagery, as competing groups of citizens strongly insist not on their commonality as Americans, but on their distinct moral, ethnic, racial, religious, and cultural identities.[39]

The American political project has historically been committed to *E pluribus unum*. Out of many peoples, traditions, languages, and cultures to create a common republic, a unified national community. We Americans shared allegiance to a common language, to representative democracy and the bill of rights, and to the cultural convictions of our Puritan and civic republican ancestors. But the suspicion and critique of political authority, and the economic, racial, and cultural diversity of our country have eroded the grip of these earlier allegiances. It is hard to resist the impression that the commonality defining us as Americans today is primarily commercial in nature.

We are individual merchants and consumers, who meet, when we do meet, in places of commerce and entertainment, like malls and stadiums. We are rarely cooperative citizens, joining together in the shared work of democratic self-government. For most of us, the government is "they," not "we," for we are autonomous individuals, defined by narrower identities, and we must be about our private or group centered business. And this fragmentation of our civic community is only intensified by the deliberate use of social media to discredit political opponents, spread lies about public challenges and policies, and generate racial, ethnic, and cultural resentment about our fellow Americans.

What should be, what can be, the unifying democratic faith in a dynamic and pluralistic democracy like ours? Galston believes that our civic aspirations should be modest, that we should accept a weak conception of citizenship. Expecting too much from our civic peers, already alienated from politics and faithful to other personal allegiances, will only be divisive and disappointing. We should limit the obligations of citizenship to the bare essentials: obeying the law, supporting our families, paying our fair share of public expenses, refraining from violence and coercive activity. Within this narrow frame of civic requirements, we should leave maximal room for personal, moral, religious, and cultural diversity.[40]

By contrast, civic republican thinkers, like Michael Sandel and Charles Taylor, believe that a much stronger conception of citizenship is needed if a new movement for economic, environmental, and political justice is to emerge and be successful. Effectively mobilizing coalitions of citizens to contend successfully with economic anxiety, pervasive injustice in the distribution of the nation's benefits and burdens, the despotic power of special interests, deliberate lies and propaganda, and the complex demands of climate change and a global economy will require moral and civic energies and coalitions that are presently in short supply. To achieve the democratic justice, that Tocqueville once lauded as the greatness and beauty of America, we need to restore an ethic of civic solidarity and mutual obligation that contemporary America does little to cultivate and much to discourage.

Recreating this unifying ethic and the cooperative action it deliberately fosters is an essential step, I believe, in overcoming our democratic discontents and restoring a warranted pride in the greatness and beauty of our country. An essential part of this critical retrieval will be restoring the vitality and benefits of liberal education for all of our citizens, no matter where they are from or now live.

NOTES

1. An excellent summary of the merits and dangers of American democracy is given in Chapters VII and VIII of Book 4, Volume II.

2. We now call this constellation of voluntary associations "civil society." Its importance in sustaining democratic liberty has not diminished with time.

3. Tocqueville's thoughtful account of "democratic individualism" can be found in Book 2, Volume II, chapters 2–4.

4. For the specific dangers of "democratic despotism," see *Democracy in America*, Volume I, Chapter XV.

5. For the sources of liberty in democratic America, see Volume I, Chapters XVI and XVII.

6. Tocqueville was deeply familiar with Montesquieu's *Spirit of the Laws*.

7. I'm summarizing here Tocqueville's extended argument in Chapters XVI and XVII of Volume I.

8. See William Galston, "Political Economy and the Politics of Virtue: US Public Philosophy at Century's End," chapter 4 in *Debating Democracy's Discontents* (New York: Oxford University Press, 1998). See also Galston's *Anti-Pluralism* (New Haven: Yale University Press, 2018). There are many important books about the state of American democracy today. I chose Galston's account because it clearly identifies so many of the salient challenges we face.

9. A likely outcome that Lyndon Johnson, a native Texan, had foreseen when the landmark civil rights bills were passed in 1964 and 1965.

10. It's important to acknowledge the many leveled causality behind this historic change.

11. So much so that Bill Clinton, the first Democratic president after Reagan (1992–2000), openly declared, "The era of big government is over." Many progressive critics of Clinton argue that his economic policies were explicitly neo-liberal in character. His support for Nafta in particular.

12. Though many of the "populists" in Trump's political coalition clearly do not favor privatizing Social Security, Medicare, and other federal assistance programs. Trump's coalition, like many before it, is a strange amalgam of "populists," economic libertarians, Christian conservatives, and racially anxious working-class whites.

13. See Galston, 65–74. I have borrowed his explanatory categories in this section of the chapter.

14. After World War II, American policy makers saw international trade as a source of global unity among traditional national rivals. But in the twenty-first century, global trade is often used as a foreign policy weapon, deepening, not alleviating, international disputes. Moreover, the strong advocates of unrestricted free trade often neglect the high human and social costs of globalization on the poor and working class.

15. The economic decline of the white working class, and their sense that neither national political party had really intervened to protect them, has been a major source of the populism Trump's "America First" rhetoric has exploited. But Trump's is a highly selective "populism," rooted in white solidarity rather than shared economic distress with blacks and working-class immigrants.

16. The scope of these economic, social, and educational disparities has been dramatically highlighted during the very long Covid pandemic.

17. The profound disruptions caused by the pandemic have reenergized the labor movement in the United States. How effective and enduring these new organizing efforts will be remains to be seen.

18. One of the deep tensions within the MAGA coalition is between its libertarian and "populist" factions. One of the strong bonds holding them together is their shared antagonism to "Democratic educational and cultural elites" whom they perceive as arrogant and self-serving.

19. One of the great challenges facing all liberal democracies is how to preserve the many benefits of global trade while protecting those harmed by it economically and socially. Both the benefits and costs of global trade must be openly acknowledged and addressed. In this very complex process, far sighted and comprehensive realism is essential. See William Galston's *Anti-Pluralism: The Populist Threat to Liberal Democracy* (New Haven: Yale University Press, 2018).

20. This reliance on scapegoats is deliberately encouraged by the lying and disinformation campaigns of the "conservative right." The political challenge is also compounded by the major transformations required to address climate change responsibly. Yet another case where great economic, political, and cultural changes create especially difficult national challenges, particularly in a deeply divided nation.

21. I am much less sanguine than Galston was, writing twenty-four years earlier, that we can find effective democratic responses to these interwoven challenges in contemporary America.

22. This is a decline thoughtfully examined by Charles Taylor, Robert Putnam, Michael Sandel, and George Packer.

23. Tocqueville, *Democracy in America*, Volume II, Book II, Chapters IV, V, VI and VII.

24. They also serve, as I have argued throughout this book, as essential sources of civic education for all citizens.

25. A genuinely free and humane society cultivates and recognizes many important human goods beyond the political and the economic.

26. See *Democracy in America*, Vol II, Book II, Chapters II-V.

27. These internal dangers to American democracy all converged in the insurrection at the Capitol on January 6, 2021, when Trump and his deliberately aroused supporters sought to overturn the legitimate election results of the previous November's presidential election.

28. For a cultural analysis of this troubling domination, see Chapter 7 in this book.

29. An impartial, independent, and respected judiciary is an essential contributor to democratic liberty and justice. An ideologically biased judiciary, by contrast, is a clear and present danger to a free and fair liberal democracy.

30. Partisans on the left see that elite as primarily economic and financial; partisans on the right see it as educational, cultural, and "globalist" in outlook. Either way, the fierce critique of and hostility to "elites" has become another divisive source of our political distress. See Michael Sandel, *The Tyranny of Merit*.

31. It remains painfully unclear what the phrase "we the people" actually means in America today. I'm thinking especially about the deep partisan divisions in the understanding and appraisal of the insurrection of January 6.

32. The sources of that trouble are far reaching, but in this book, I've emphasized especially our grave failures in civic education. Failures that affect and limit democratic leaders, democratic political parties, and democratic citizens.

33. Charles Taylor's work is masterful in distinguishing and then integrating the intellectual, moral, and spiritual sources of our distress. See especially *Sources of the Self, A Secular Age, and The Ethics of Authenticity*.

34. This is one of the most important but least thoughtfully discussed problems of our time.

35. Yet another reason for the importance of civic education and a genuinely liberal education for democratic citizens everywhere.

36. See *Democracy in America*, Volume I, Chapter XVII.

37. Contemporary "Christian Nationalists" seek to restore the cultural and political primacy of a "traditionalist understanding of Christianity" within contemporary America. But this goal is inconsistent with our constitutional understanding of religious liberty. For a very different understanding of our existing religious pluralism, see Charles Taylor's *A Secular Age*.

38. See Tocqueville, *Democracy in America*, Volume I, Chapter XVIII.

39. Though a common civic identity is fully consistent with religious, ethnic, and racial pluralism.

40. See Galston, 67–85.

Chapter 7

The Cultural Struggle for American Democracy

"It is the justice of democracy that constitutes its greatness and beauty."

Alexis De Tocqueville, *Democracy in America*, II, 349–52

What does it mean to be an American citizen today? What will it take to protect and preserve a government of, by, and for the people, 160 years after Lincoln voiced these high hopes for our democracy? And why have so many Americans become distrustful of government, suspicious of politics, and uncertain of their own civic obligations? These are the important questions I seek to explore in this extended political and cultural reflection.

In responding to these questions, I want to take a longer view than that normally offered in contemporary political commentary. For me, these questions are fundamentally cultural; they concern deep cultural changes that often take centuries to evolve and solidify. The purpose of this reflection is to uncover the profound civic implications of important cultural changes within American democracy over the last 250 years.

In my judgment, the most powerful forces at work in our society today are anti-political.[1] Their domination of our public life helps to explain the erosion of political authority and the sad state of civic engagement and trust. But what deeper cultural changes underlie and sustain these troubling signs of democratic unrest? If we agree with Charles Taylor that a healthy American democracy requires creating a never stable balance between political and economic concerns and anxieties, between the democratic struggle for equal liberty and justice and the capitalist struggle for personal profit and security, how did it happen that the acquisitive spirit of capitalism became so deeply entrenched in our public life, and that the traditional authority of politics over economics was almost completely reversed?[2]

POLITICS: THE CIVIC REPUBLICAN VIEW

In her memorable study of America's founding, Hannah Arendt describes "the lost treasure of the American Revolution."[3] That treasure, which grew out of the American colonial experience of limited self-government, was based on three complementary principles. *Civic virtue*, which meant consistently putting the public good before private interests. *Political liberty*, which meant regular, active, and informed participation by citizens in the project of republican self-government. And *public happiness*, which meant the shared enjoyment citizens discovered in the responsible conduct of public affairs. These complementary principles are essential to the political convictions and conduct of the founding generation that created our constitutional republic.[4]

But, according to Arendt, they were neglected, forgotten, or deliberately rejected during the long nineteenth century, so that a critical part of our American political inheritance remains largely unknown today. In the following cultural and political reflection, I am seeking to recover important public goods that we have collectively lost or forgotten.

What are the core elements in the civic republican understanding of politics? And why have we collectively failed to remember and enact our "*lost public treasure*"?

The Enduring Bond of Human Beings in Political Communities:

There are many purposes for which human beings unite and act cooperatively. There are many partial interests that hold them together and separate them from rival groups with opposing practical agendas. Distinctively political associations are ways of being and living together in which citizens are united by a self and group transcending love that entails mutual obligations and shared responsibilities. This may be love of the world, devotion to equal justice, shared allegiance to country, an explicit commitment to protecting and advancing the common good, or the passionate desire to share as free citizens in responsible self-government. These unifying civic loves are typically combined with a hatred of despotism, or arbitrary self-interested rule, in all its forms.[5] The civic republican vision of politics rests on the shared conviction that all citizens are free deliberative agents capable of directing their community's affairs and providing responsibly for the basic needs of future generations ("our fiduciary obligations to posterity").[6]

The Dignity of The Public Realm

Because of their inherent complexity, human beings have both private and public concerns. To address their private concerns, they rely on marriage and the family, extended kinship relations, the fellowship of friends, and a broad range of voluntary associations. In the intermediate zone between family and government lies civil society. The voluntary associations constituting civil society pursue both private and public goods. While the agents of government are public officials charged with protecting and advancing the common good, the character of contemporary civil society is less clearly defined. Religious communities, colleges and universities, labor unions, business corporations, public charities, a broad range of non-profits, and a plethora of interest groups have both public and private dimensions. While serving the needs and aims of their members, their decisions and actions clearly affect the common world to which all citizens belong.

The growth and complexity of American civil society have made a sharp public/private separation untenable today. Still, it remains critical to distinguish between acting for the sake of one's own (family, group, limited and partial interests) and acting for the benefit of the comprehensive and enduring political community.[7] I agree with Arendt that a distinctively political mentality should be adopted when engaged in the public realm. She calls this cast of mind "an enlarged mentality" that enables citizens to rise above their limited and partisan interests and perspectives in order to speak, decide, and act together for the common good.[8]

To achieve and maintain an enlarged mentality, citizens must be free from the urgent demands of biological necessity, as well as partisan attachment to the circumscribed ends of self or group. The dignity of the public realm rests on each citizen's capacity to rise above private need and partisan interests, to deliberate, decide, and act for the whole community; and to find public happiness and joy in caring for the world with our peers. One of the essential aims of a liberal education is actively to cultivate such an enlarged mentality in all of our citizens.[9]

The Intrinsic Importance of Speech and Action

What do citizens do when they enter the public realm to enact the affairs of the world? Essentially, they speak with one another; they converse. But their incessant discussion is guided by a more important purpose: to promote and preserve the present and future well-being of the entire political community. The civic republican conception of the public or common good is not amorphous. As clearly articulated in the Preamble to the United States Constitution, the public good includes strengthening our political union, establishing justice and national peace, promoting public prosperity, and securing the blessings of personal and public liberty for future generations. When free citizens deliberate and debate, when they decide and act in concert, and when they reflect critically on the intended and unintended consequences of their actions, these are among the public goods they hope to define and achieve together.[10]

Because the political realm is open to a broad plurality of citizens, each with his/her own opinions and judgments; because its transactions are based on persuasion and argument, rather than personal authority or coercive force; and because political agents are fallible and often shortsighted, our personal conception of the common good and of the best ways to achieve it may not often prevail. But our failure to achieve the policy objectives we support does not mean that our speech and action were futile. Political achievement should never be measured by a narrow calculus of victories and defeats. By acting with consistent integrity in the political give and take, by respecting the rights and opinions of our peers, and by remaining politically committed in the face of inevitable setbacks and disappointments, we help to keep the public realm open and free. We also create bonds of solidarity and mutual respect with both those who support and oppose our political arguments and judgments.[11]

In this critical sense, there are no "winners and losers" in genuinely republican politics. The language and metaphors of competitive sports, so prominent in the media's commentary on politics, do not really apply in this essentially cooperative domain. Teaching young citizens to think and speak responsibly about politics and political activity is another important goal of a liberal education. Learning how to cooperate effectively across significant differences is one of the enduring benefits of a sound education.

The Complementarity of Common Sense and Practical Reason

There is a strong cognitive dimension to civic republican politics. Sound public policies emerge through thoughtfully integrating three forms of knowledge: factual knowledge of the world as it is and has been; evaluative knowledge of the specific goods and norms appropriate to a political democracy; deliberative knowledge of the best way to achieve those goods and respect those norms in the concrete and changing conditions of practical life.

These complementary forms of knowledge are, in principle, available to all informed citizens. It is the political community's responsibility, and that of liberal arts colleges especially, to educate their citizens in these distinct forms of collaborative knowledge. And it is the individual citizen's, and student's, responsibility, in turn, to acquire and exercise the range of knowledge required by our common political vocation. In America today, the level of civic ignorance, historical amnesia, moral confusion, pervasive disinformation, and deliberately divisive lying is a source of profound public shame and distress.[12]

Public Liberty

> "Those things we must learn before we can do them, we learn by doing them."
>
> Aristotle, *Nicomachean Ethics*.[13]

The concept of public or political liberty is at the core of civic republicanism. Political liberty requires abundant opportunities for citizens to share in the conduct of public affairs. It means the freedom to engage directly through participation, and indirectly through representation, in political life: to deliberate, to evaluate, to decide, and act in concert with our peers in determining public policy and law. Public liberty is supported by a sound civic education, township government, freedom of assembly and association, the right to petition for redress of grievances, the regular accountability of elected officials, the freedom, independence and good judgment of the press, the responsible exercise of public dissent and criticism.

Tocqueville repeatedly emphasized the importance of public liberty for a sound and vibrant democracy. "The only effective remedy for the evils of democratic equality is political or public liberty."[14] But he cautioned that political liberty is easily lost, often neglected, and regularly avoided in democratic cultures. Aristocratic in origin and spirit, and in permanent conflict with the democratic passions for wealth and material comfort, public liberty requires an extended civic apprenticeship in "grammar schools of liberty."

The rights of citizenship alone do not guarantee the reality of political freedom, an acquired set of public habits and virtues that only develop through repeated experience in exchanging informed opinions and responsibly debating contested judgments with our civic peers. Through conversing responsibly and openly with other citizens, we enlarge our minds to understand their opinions and judgments, and we enlarge our hearts to appreciate their hopes, sorrows, and fears. These indispensable political arts and virtues only flourish in a democratic community that deliberately promotes the liberal education of all its citizens through factual and historical knowledge, informed discussion and dialogue, and responsible cooperative action.[15]

But in modern liberal democracies, the great majority of citizens deliberately avoid the public realm and view with suspicion the "politicians" who enter it. The dominant ideology of market capitalism promotes a narrow attachment to private interests, and most citizens tolerate a demoralizing public realm if their individual interests and rights are reliably protected.[16]

But why have these core elements of civic republicanism (love of the world, and of the distinctive joys of cooperative and responsible public engagement; the recognized dignity of free speech, action, deliberative reasoning and common sense; the intrinsic value of political agents, events and communities; the democratic treasure of public liberty) become forgotten, neglected, or openly rejected after the American Revolution had run its course? There are many reasons this invaluable public treasure largely disappeared, but in this chapter, I want to identify the specifically economic reasons that largely account for our common loss.[17]

THE IMPERIAL ASSUMPTIONS OF ECONOMICS

Economic practice and theory deeply informed the cultural outlook of Western Modernity. By the nineteenth century, a radical set of assumptions about human existence became widely accepted in "enlightened circles," particularly among the founders of the new human sciences. I shall refer to these reductive anthropological prejudices as the "imperial assumptions of economics." It is important to note that these ruling assumptions spanned the familiar oppositions among economic theorists, uniting, rather than dividing, classical liberals and their socialist rivals.

What are these assumptions, and what has been their reductive effect on the American understanding of education, politics, and citizenship?

The True Basis of All Human Association Is Economic

The most important reason human beings join in cooperative activity is for the production, distribution, use, and consumption of material goods. All other human purposes are subordinate to the preservation and extension of individual and species life.[18]

The Underlying Motive of All Human Activity is Self-Interest

It is the pursuit of material advantage that drives the behavior of individuals, groups, and social classes. Normative appeals to disinterested and principled action are either hypocritical or naïve. Such high-minded appeals actually serve as a veil for self-interest, as a deliberate or unconscious strategy for duping the gullible or pacifying the oppressed. Moreover, ostensibly disinterested activity is not the true cause of advancing the common good. For classical liberals, there is an "invisible hand" at work in the marketplace, creating public prosperity from the passionate pursuit of private gain. For their Marxist adversaries, the dialectical laws of history will ultimately generate a classless society from the historical antagonism of rival class-based economic interests. What really drives human progress is not the free and responsible actions of informed citizens, but impersonal economic laws, the laws of the unregulated market, or the dialectical laws of class struggle.

Human Beings, Therefore, Are Essentially Economic Animals

We rise above the other animals through the rational dimension of our economic activities. We use "calculative reason," the deliberate coordination of means and ends, in producing, exchanging, distributing, and acquiring the material goods that sustain our individual and collective lives. Using "technical reason," we gradually learn to create tools and machines that increase the fecundity of the production process. With their aid, not life alone, but material abundance, physical comfort, and the partial escape from our biological needs become palpable benefits available to all.[19]

All Human Activities Are to Be Measured and Appraised in Terms of Their Productive Potential

Because genuine knowledge is assumed to be power that proves its worth through the "fruits and works" it helps to create, all non-productive modes of existence become inherently suspect.[20] The philosophical life and the life of active citizenship, the very summit of the ancient ethical hierarchy, are discredited by this "enlightened" suspicion. Theoretical contemplation, disinterested reflection and inquiry, and political words and deeds, leave nothing tangible and durable in their wake. In marked contrast, *homo faber*, the skilled craftsman, produces lasting and useful artifacts; *homo mercator*, the capitalist merchant, produces rising national wealth; and the *animal laborans*, the unskilled wage laborer, produces an abundant supply of consumable goods to sustain biological life.[21]

The classical understanding of leisure (*schole*) is also subverted by this economic vision of human existence. For classical and medieval thinkers, leisure was the basis of culture. Freed from the stern demands of necessity and utility, citizens at leisure were free for intrinsically liberal activities: prayer, meditation, worship, theoretical inquiry, the distinctive joys of friendship, intimacy, and engagement in the political life. These were the genuinely free activities in which humans exercised their very highest capacities. They encountered the divine; they delighted in the discovery of truth; they cooperated responsibly in caring for the world and their neighbors.[22]

But the modern economic mentality views these classical liberal activities as parasitic. Depending on the work and labor of others, they contribute nothing to the growth of public power and wealth. By the normative standards of modern economics, only productive activities and the steady creation of cumulative wealth are really significant. Periods of leisure are the recurrent occasions of idleness that briefly interrupt serious work. Leisure, therefore, is to be filled with relaxation, entertainment, shopping, the replenishing of energy for the really serious business of economic life.

The Cultural Revision of *"Noblesse Oblige"*

Throughout Western history, the dominant economic class had always assumed the obligations of political leadership. This was true of the slave societies of ancient Greece and the feudal societies of medieval Europe. Until the European nobility lost their political independence to the absolute monarchs, the claims of *"noblesse oblige"* remained in force. But the subsequent rise of the bourgeoisie in the eighteenth and nineteenth centuries was marked by explicitly anti-political prejudices. This newly dominant economic class eagerly embraced the ideology of *laissez-faire.*[23]

Merchants, bankers, industrialists, and traders insisted on freedom from government interference and regulation, so that they could energetically pursue economic gain. What the bourgeoisie demanded from government was security: the protection of their lives, families, property, and investments, with the guarantee of unimpeded economic liberty. Since the "invisible hand" would reliably promote the public good, government activity should be minimal and non-intrusive, particularly in the economic realm. It was the titans of commerce, finance, and industry, not the political leaders and representatives of the state, who ensured real national progress.

In this historic cultural reversal, first, politics became subordinate to economics, the deliberative assembly to the capitalist marketplace. Then politics itself was transformed into a type of business, democratic citizens into consumers, political speech into public relations, reasoned argument into emotional bumper stickers intended to manipulate unreflective emotions, rather than to inform, persuade, and unite thoughtful minds. The political media became fascinated by the incessant competition among partisan factions, mindlessly reporting who's winning or losing the intense political struggle for increased market share (our uncritical fascination with public opinion polls).[24]

There is, today, no shortage of public speech, but too much of it is mind-numbing chatter, deliberate lying or partisan propaganda, that utterly fails the enduring test of political discourse: to illumine, to inspire, to inform, and to teach responsible citizens about the true condition of the world, and of the public challenges we must address cooperatively together.[25]

THE STRUGGLE FOR DEMOCRATIC JUSTICE

Can the reductive grip of these one-sided cultural and political prejudices be broken?[26] Can American democracy recover its original and energizing civic republican spirit? The deepest reforms we require today are intellectual, moral, and cultural. At every level of our divided society, Americans need to reexamine the ways we think, speak, and feel about education, citizenship, government, and the human good. We have created a public culture that emphasizes individual rights and neglects public responsibilities; that celebrates the pursuit of self-interest and casts suspicion on the great civic virtues; that highlights individual misconduct and glosses over systemic injustice, and that cultivates skeptical distrust and suspicion of the collaborative discovery and achievement of the common good.

Credible political reforms must be guided by the imperative of equal justice. Public confidence in democratic governments rests on the confirmed belief that the needs and concerns of all citizens are accorded equal weight, that the concrete requirements of true political equality are actually met. Citizens must also be convinced that political and economic power are fairly distributed and responsibly balanced; and that public officials, at all levels of government, remain independent of the organized interests they are intended to oversee and to regulate.[27]

Justice also requires an equitable distribution of the benefits and burdens of social cooperation.[28] The regulative principle in a modern democracy is civic equality: equality under the law, equality of education and opportunity, and equal treatment and respect in the different sectors of institutional life. But democratic equality is, in practice, complex. Where no relevant distinction is made among the claims of individual citizens, the appropriate form of equality is arithmetic: for example, equality of individual rights and liberties, and equality of political representation (one person, one vote). But in those domains where genuine differences of merit exist among citizens, the appropriate form of equality is geometric or proportional.

In distributing public benefits, such as honors, offices, and income, those who contribute more to the collective good are entitled to receive more in return. BUT the benefits they receive should always be proportionate to their specific contributions. The same principle applies to the sharing of public burdens, such as taxation or military service. Those citizens better able to carry the relevant burden should carry the heavier load. Everyone should contribute in accordance with his/her ability and resources; no one should carry an inordinate share; but to whom much is given, much should be expected in return.

Political solidarity in a modern democracy depends on achieving economic, political, educational, and social justice. There should be an equitable distribution of wealth, income, education, opportunity, and economic security, with guarantees of a decent minimum for all. Scandalous inequality in the distribution of public goods and obligations is profoundly divisive. Politically, it erodes public trust in the legitimacy of both government and business. Educationally, it tends to create serious and demoralizing cultural and political rifts within the democratic electorate. Socially, it promotes dangerous cycles of poverty, addiction, alienation, and crime. The radical and deepening inequality of wealth and income in the United States, and the warranted fear that economic and educational inequalities translate directly into massive political inequality (including "dark money," voter suppression, partisan gerrymandering, the massive and dishonest lobbying industry) raise credible alarms about the integrity and justice of our communal life.[29]

These justice centered concerns are relevant to all citizens: to public officials, the press, lobbyists and political consultants, teachers, scholars, critics, parents, to the entire people as members of the common political whole. Restoring political soundness to our democracy and strengthening our fractured political union are shared responsibilities. Correcting serious failures in democratic justice will require individual, institutional, and cultural changes. Individuals will need to think, speak, and act like responsible citizens, rather than petitioning consumers. Structural inequities in our political, educational, and economic institutions will need to be remedied through substantive reforms in policy, practice, and law. And the domination of our civic culture by the capitalist values of self-interest and unbridled competition will need to be deliberately reversed by a comprehensive commitment to civic virtues, public liberty, and the common good. In creating and sustaining that commitment over time, a liberal education for all citizens must play an indispensable role.

The great challenges to the American democratic experiment differ from generation to generation. We are not called today to create a new constitution, to end slavery, or to resist the totalitarian menace of Nazism and Stalinism. The grave challenge we face is to recreate economic justice, political solidarity, and responsible civic minded participation in a global society marked by scandalous inequities, rampant disinformation, and new forms of ideology and terror.

The lost treasure of the American Revolution was the unifying democratic spirit of shared sacrifice, civic solidarity, and responsible deliberative engagement. Unless we recover that original spirit in a new and revitalized form, our democratic discontents are certain to deepen and multiply. But in restoring and renewing that revolutionary spirit, we would also help to restore politics, authentic democratic politics, to its rightful place among the great human goods that we commonly, honor, remember, and prize.[30]

NOTES

1. My understanding of politics is based on three complementary realities: my experience of American citizenship and active political deliberation for the last sixty-five years; the civic republican tradition that emphasizes the civic virtue of citizens, their responsible exercise of public liberty, and their enduring commitment to the common good as the goal of political deliberation and choice; and the social justice teachings of gospel inspired Christianity.

2. See "Political Fragmentation," the final essay in Charles Taylor's *Ethics of Authenticity*.

3. See Hannah Arendt's *On Revolution*, chapter 6, "The Revolutionary Tradition and its Lost Treasure."

4. For a comprehensive articulation and defense of these principles, see Michael McCarthy, *The Political Humanism of Hannah Arendt*.

5. For the classical analysis of despotism in contrast to political legitimacy, see Aristotle's *Politics*, Book III, chapters 6–13.

6. A central theme in both the Declaration of Independence and the Preamble to the United States Constitution.

7. Both of these attributes are essential to determining "the common good." *Comprehensive*, the common good extends to the whole political community; *enduring*, it looks to the foreseeable future as well as the present.

8. See Hannah Arendt, *Lectures on Kant's Political Philosophy* (Chicago: University of Chicago Press, 1982) 43.

9. For an elaboration and defense of civic republicanism, see *Civic Republicanism*, Iseult Honohan (London: Routledge, 2002).

10. The common good is historically sensitive and situation specific, so that the range of public goods it encompasses is generally larger than this enumerated set.

11. These are among the public virtues citizens regularly acquire in what Tocqueville calls "grammar schools of liberty." See *Democracy in America*. But sadly, their prominent absence from contemporary political debate and argument makes it increasingly shrill, demoralizing, and ineffective.

12. As I argue in chapter 1, there are many sources of division within American democracy, but the important cognitive failures, factual, moral, and deliberative, are among the most crippling. All three of these failures point to underlying weaknesses in our civic and cultural education, as well as the demagogic practices of both the right and the left.

13. In the *Nicomachean Ethics*, Aristotle draws an important distinction between "doing what the virtuous person does" and "doing it as the virtuous person does it." Though we learn by doing in acquiring the arts, it is only when we've actually mastered the arts, that we fully enjoy what we've learned.

14. *Democracy in America*, Volume I, chapter 5.

15. The "schools of liberty," the places where we acquire the political arts and virtues, are meant to complement each other. Township government, voluntary associations, liberal arts colleges, even public-spirited religious communities all should play a role in the civic formation of responsible citizens. One important way to measure the health of American democracy today is to determine whether they actually do this, or even try to.

16. A recurrent example of the priority of self-interest over the common good.

17. Gordon Wood's book, *The Radicalism of the American Revolution*, offers an historical account of this dramatic shift in America's public priorities.

18. A very important influence on these anthropological prejudices was Charles Darwin's theory of evolution. Particularly its principle of "the survival of the fittest" in the interspecies struggle for survival.

19. The contrast between "calculative reason," "technical reason," and "deliberative practical reason" is an important part of the cultural narrative I am recounting. When politics has authority over economics, then practical wisdom determines the scope and range of both calculative and technical reason.

20. Francis Bacon, *Novum Organon*, "For fruits and works are as it were sponsors and sureties for the truth of philosophies."

21. For the important distinction between "the animal laborans," "homo mercator," and "homo faber," see Hannah Arendt's *The Human Condition.*

22. Though writing sixteen hundred years after Aristotle, Aquinas incorporates these hierarchical principles into his synoptic theological vision. Both Aristotle and Aquinas accept the traditional distinction between the necessary, the useful and the liberal.

23. For the reductive ideology at the heart of classical economic liberalism, see chapter 3.

24. Even "serious political commentary" operates within this narrow and distorted understanding of the "political," as the incessant struggle for public power to advance and protect private interest(s).

25. For useful background to these modern economic developments and attitudes, see Robert Heilbroner, *The Worldly Philosophers* (New York: Simon and Schuster, 1986).

26. "The only lost cause is one we give up before we enter the struggle." See Vaclav Havel, *Summer Meditations* (New York: Random House, 1993).

27. But we must frankly acknowledge that from the time of our founding, these democratic ideals have never been achieved in our political practice. For this reason, the historical narratives we share with our students must be grounded in "critical belonging," recognizing both the power of democratic ideals and our collective failure to honor them in practice.

28. A formulation borrowed from John Rawls' *A Theory of Justice.*

29. See *The Ethics of Lobbying* (Washington DC: Georgetown University Press).

30. See "Is there a Way to Get There from Here?" the concluding reflection in *The Political Humanism of Hannah Arendt.*

Chapter 8

Our Search for Wisdom

The Stories We Live By

"Compare our nature in respect of education and its lack to such an experience as this. Picture men dwelling in a sort of subterranean cave. . . . with
their legs and necks fettered from childhood." "A strange image you speak
of with strange prisoners." "Like us, he said."

Plato, *The Republic*, 514a–15a.

Thinking about the nature and purpose of education forces us to examine
permanent philosophical concerns. My goal in this chapter is to reflect on an
important set of those concerns, which I connect in the following pattern. The
primary goal of education is to cultivate specific virtues or excellences that
human beings would otherwise not possess. These virtues are indispensable
if human beings are to become effectively free. This condition of developed
or actualized freedom, once achieved, prepares us for responsible and effective engagement in the many different communities to which we belong.
Or, to put the same point in negative terms: if education fails in its primary
purpose, then important virtues remain undeveloped, effective freedom is
not achieved, and our mature engagement in communal life will, at best, be
half-hearted and self-serving.

The literature of education is full of memorable stories in which contrasting views of human nature and the human condition are writ large, and in
which the themes of this chapter hold a central place. I shall reflect on a
few of these well-preserved stories, occasionally stopping to comment upon
them, and to make explicit some of the contested truth-claims they express.
After recounting these tales, I shall shift expository levels and articulate some
conceptual connections between liberal education and the goal of effective
freedom; connections that, I believe, are extremely significant if they are true.

Then I shall tell a final story, not my own, but a story in which I believe, that suggests how we might learn to live without wisdom, even as we actively search for it.

The first story, taken from Plato's dialogue *Protagoras*, was told to Socrates by the great sophist, Protagoras of Abdera, during his heralded visit to Athens.[1] It is a myth about the origin, nature, and development of human beings. Like other creation stories, it has a familiar beginning. Once upon a time, there were only gods and no mortals. But the gods had decided to create mortals by fashioning them out of the earth. They assigned the task of allocating natural capacities to these new creatures to two of their peers, Epimetheus and Prometheus. Epimetheus was eager to begin, and so he asked Prometheus to let him do the work alone, though Prometheus could check the results once Epimetheus had finished. As a good naturalist, Epimetheus allocated natural powers in accord with the principle of compensation. Since he wanted all the mortal species to survive (he was clearly not a Darwinian), he balanced the strength of one species against the weakness of another. So, he gave to some creatures strength without speed, and to others speed without strength. To some, he gave size without great mobility, but to the small, mobility with the added power of concealment. In allocating skin and hair, the distribution of edible foods, as well as rates of fertility, he followed religiously the compensatory design of species survival.[2]

But Epimetheus was not a particularly clever person, as his Greek name meaning *hindsight* implies, so that he used up the available natural capacities on the beasts before he had provided anything for humans. When Prometheus came to investigate Epimetheus' work, he found men and women naked, unshod, unprotected, and unarmed. At a loss initially about how to ensure human survival, Prometheus eventually stole from the gods the gift of skill in the arts together with the controlled use of fire. Through these gifts, humans gained the means of survival, but Prometheus, due to the oversight of his impetuous colleague, later had to stand trial before the gods for his theft.[3]

After humans first appeared on the earth, they lived originally in scattered groups; there were no cities, no political communities then. But in this apolitical condition, they still proved weaker than many of the beasts. So, eventually, they began to band together in political communities for the sake of mutual protection. Yet, because they lacked the political arts, the arts of shared deliberation, discussion and compromise, they regularly injured one another and struggled to live amicably together. Zeus, the chief among the Olympian gods, fearing, like Prometheus, for their survival, then sent Hermes, his messenger, to bestow upon humans the political arts of respect for others, and a sense of justice and lawful order, so that they might dwell together in peace. Although the individual potential for achieving skill in the arts was not distributed equally, Hermes was instructed to give everyone a share in the political virtues, since lacking them, humans could not live together in concord.[4]

In his commentary on the myth, Protagoras claims that nature has not been generous to human beings, leaving them incomplete and unequipped for the demands of mortal life. To complete their nature, to ensure their survival, and to make possible a life beyond mere necessity, humans need to acquire specific arts and virtues to compensate for what nature has left unfinished. In Protagoras' explanatory account, two kinds of arts are identified: (1) The technical arts, which enable humans to cope with the many challenges of nature and thus survive; and (2) the political arts, which enable them to live peacefully in groups while pursuing their personal and communal interests. Education is described by Protagoras as a means of developing and exercising these different but complementary arts. In its most advanced form, education produces two types of expert: first, the craftsman, or specialist, in technical knowledge, like the carpenter, the hunter, or the medical doctor; and second, the statesman, an expert in the effective and peaceful conduct of public affairs.[5]

For Protagoras, education, from birth onward, is a continuous training in the skills needed for survival and human cooperation. In its advanced form, it enables human beings with greater natural ability and more effective educations to achieve positions of eminence or leadership among their peers. At this level, education becomes competitive, as ambitious members of the city strive for greatness and public recognition by surpassing their civic peers in technical or political achievement. I'm often led to compare Protagoras' educational ideal to the meritocratic *ethos* of a contemporary Ivy League college.[6]

Socrates' subsequent interrogation of Protagoras highlights an ambiguity in Protagoras' notion of statesmanship or political virtue. For Protagoras, the specific art of the politician is skill in effective persuasion. They are able to propose and defend public policies which the other citizens will accept and enact. This skill, in which the statesman specializes, is rhetoric or public oratory, and the knowledge he has mastered is knowing how to shape and command public opinion. Protagoras' statesman, however, does not know what is actually good for the city and its people, but he does know what most of the citizens believe is good, and what they will accept or refuse in the way of public policy and law. This developed skill, the acquired capacity to cultivate loyalty and influence people's opinions, strikes Socrates as something less than genuine political virtue. And the dialogue concludes in an apparent impasse between the two men, with Socrates insisting that genuine political virtue is based on knowledge of what is really good, while Protagoras, the sophist, contends that political virtue can be taught by paid rhetoricians like himself, even though it is not based on actual knowledge of the good.[7]

I'll conclude the first story at this point, though I shall return to its central themes in my later reflection. The second story is a distinctively modern story rather than an ancient one. It is a myth recounted by Jean Jacques Rousseau in his *Second Discourse on the Origin of Inequality*. It is a myth intended to make intelligible a basic principle in which Rousseau deeply believed. Namely, the radical social principle "That man is born free, but now finds himself everywhere in chains."[8] Like Protagoras' myth, Rousseau's story presents human beings in their *original* condition, which for Rousseau is our *natural* condition. Rousseau calls this original human condition the "state of Nature," and he calls the individual human member of this state "the natural man" or the "noble savage."[9]

What are humans really like by nature? According to Rousseau, our original condition is one of solitude; each person lives alone. There are two common principles that dictate human conduct in this solitary condition: first, the desire for self-preservation, for the survival of the self; and second, the sentiment of compassion. The first principle means that each human has a natural or innate aversion to his/her suffering or death. The second principle means that each has a natural aversion to witnessing the suffering of others. For Rousseau, the first natural principle takes precedence over the second, as the individual will injure others to protect him/her self, but will not inflict suffering gratuitously. Taken together, these two principles constitute, for Rousseau, the primary ethical maxim, a maxim strikingly different from the traditional golden rule of human activity, "Do unto others as you would have them do unto you." Rousseau's ethical rule is, rather "Do good to yourself, with as little evil to others as possible."[10] Everything you do or say is all right, as long as other people don't get hurt.

How does the solitary individual spend her time in the state of nature? Mostly in eating, drinking, sleeping, and when nature urges, engaging in transient and impersonal sexual activity . . . a particularly vivid case of solitary strangers passing in the night. Rousseau pictures nature as an abundant and largely uninhabited forest in which individuals can survive, even be happy, without reliance on labor, art, science, thinking or the continuing companionship of others.[11] The natural individual is a creature of sensibility and temporal immediacy, entirely lacking in innate intellectual capacity. A being spared the emotions of fear and regret that are rooted in the sense of time, the individual human lives entirely in the present, enjoying the delightful experience of simply being alive. For the natural man or woman, mere *existence feels good*. The noble savage is a being who receives no education and needs no education, that is, needs no education in order to be free, happy, virtuous, and independent. We can better understand these unorthodox claims, as well as the larger purpose of the myth, if we stop to clarify Rousseau's basic terms.

For Rousseau, humans are naturally asocial beings with no inherent need or desire for community. In stark contrast to the ancient Greeks, Rousseau denies that humans are by nature political animals. For him, the history of human society, of humans living together in stable groups, has been largely a history of bondage. Society constantly ensnares natural men and women in invisible nets, the nets of family, country, church, school, or communal institutions generally. Society robs individuals of their natural independence and sovereignty by arousing in them unnatural desires that they need the aid of others to satisfy. It robs individuals of their natural sense of immediacy, of their innate spontaneity, by developing in them a rational life that is unnatural and obstructive of immediate feeling. Most seriously, life in society, robs them of the happiness, freedom, and goodness, which they experienced naturally in their original solitary condition.[12]

But in what sense were these solitary individuals originally happy, free, and good? Rousseau's answers are straightforward and simple. The original individuals were happy because their natural desires did not outrun their natural powers. When the native powers of individuals enable them independently to satisfy their desires, they are happy. They are also free because they are entirely independent of human authority.[13] For Rousseau, humans are born free because they are born able to exercise their own wills without meeting resistance in the will of other humans. But now, they are everywhere in chains because the existing network of social obligations and responsibilities requires them to submit their wills to the wills of others. And they were originally good, not because they had cultivated and exercised the virtues, achieved excellence, or transcended self-interest through concern for the well-being of others, but because they regularly satisfied Rousseau's ethical maxim, "Do good to yourself with as little evil to others as possible." Our innate impulses toward self-preservation and compassion ensure our natural goodness without our needing to reflect and thoughtfully decide about what we should say or do.[14]

Now, Rousseau knows that this story is a myth, not a part of anthropological history (at least he usually does), and he cautions his readers that we cannot now return to our original state. He even acknowledges that the original condition is not ideal for humans, that a somewhat similar though slightly different state would be better. But in describing the natural, solitary state as happy, free, and good, he evokes an important *affective response* in his readers. Namely, the strong feeling that the energy we devote to education, to the deliberate cultivation of the arts and virtues, to the foundation and preservation of civilized communities is misplaced and unnecessary. It is the deep feeling that somehow human life should be simpler and easier, that intellectual development should be less important, that healthy self-interest tempered by spontaneous compassion is sufficient for living well; and that heroism, in both its personal and communal forms, is unnecessary since human happiness is possible without the deliberate cultivation of virtue.[15]

Rousseau's story of the natural man may, in part, have been a counterattack on earlier myths, that of Protagoras, for example, or that of Socrates in Book Seven of the *Republic* where he narrates to Glaucon, his youthful interlocutor, his memorable myth of the cave. I have always found this Platonic myth ambiguous, hard to interpret, difficult to understand fully. I assume Plato intended it as such. Let me first recount the myth as Socrates presents it, and then discuss my ambivalence about it.

The cave is an image, Socrates tells us, of human nature with respect to education and its lack.[16] We are like people who dwell in a subterranean cave with a long entrance open to the light. Beginning in childhood, we are bound, legs and necks, to a stationary position in the depth of the cave. Because of our chains, we can only look forward; we cannot turn our heads or look directly at each other. Behind us, but at a higher level, there is a light burning from a fire. Between the fire and us, the immobile prisoners, there is a road along which a low wall has been built like the partitions in a puppet show. Invisible people walk behind the wall carrying artificial objects of every kind above their heads. These objects, which are themselves images of real things, cast shadows on the wall in front of the prisoners, which are then observed by them. "A strange image and strange prisoners," Glaucon says. "Like us," Socrates replies.[17]

The bound prisoners take pleasure in assigning names to the shadows cast by the images of real things, although the prisoners assume that the shadows themselves are independently real, not simply wavering reflections of already artificial entities. Honors are distributed to those prisoners who excel in determining the sequences of precedence and co-existence among the shadows (very much like David Hume's subsequent theory of sensible impressions and ideas). Now, suppose, Socrates says, one of the prisoners were released from the bonds, were liberated from this condition of original ignorance, and were compelled to stand up and walk about in the cave.[18] At first, dazzled by the light of the fire, she would lose her bearings; her earlier sense of what was real and what was not would be greatly confused. She would initially want to return to the familiar world of shadows, within which she felt more secure. But if those who released her, dragged her forth with difficulty out of the cave into the true light of day, she would need time to habituate herself to seeing real things rather than the shadows cast by the artificial images. Only gradually, and by ordered stages of discovery, could she bear to perceive real objects, and finally to perceive the sun itself on which those objects depend for their existence and visibility.[19]

But once she had endured and become accustomed to this critical psychic conversion, this *metanoia*, this turning around of the human soul, once she had left the cave to live among visible realities beneath the sun and the sky, she would no longer want to return. Having gradually passed from darkness into light, she would not want to pass back from light into darkness. Yet in Socrates' myth, the liberated prisoner is compelled to return by those who originally released her; compelled to live again among the other prisoners, compelled for the cognitive and practical benefit of the original cave community, though now her sense of what is real and valuable is radically different from theirs. What they consider real and important are for her merely semblances of semblances of true reality. After her return, she now lives among them like a stranger, because their passionate concerns and convictions are no longer her own. She has undergone a conversion of the soul, a radical change of perspective, value, and purpose, which makes her alien to the other prisoners and arouses their hostility. They regard her as dangerous and are even prepared to kill her.[20]

Socrates partly explains the myth to Glaucon by telling him that the cave is the *sensible* realm in which we humans normally live; and that the world and sky outside the cave is *the intelligible* realm of forms, climaxing in the form of the Good, of which the sun of our regular experience is merely the visible image. The upward and downward path of the prisoner is the path of true education, which leads the liberated student from impressions, hearsay, and received opinions to genuine understanding and knowledge of the real. The initial phase of a liberal education is liberation or conversion, in which a person is released from the bonds of ignorance or false belief to begin a long process of ascent to comprehensive and genuine knowledge.[21] Liberal education, at the beginning, is particularly difficult, because those who are bound by ignorance believe themselves to be already knowledgeable and free. This belief is habitually confirmed by their fellow prisoners, while those who challenge its truth are openly threatened or rejected. Education is initially a bewildering experience in which we enter unknown terrain that, at first, seems dark to us, even though it lies directly within the light of the sun. Our impatience makes us want to see the sun directly, to know the Good, to become, in fact, rapidly wise. But were liberated cave dwellers directly confronted with the sun, they would be blinded by its powerful light, for which they are still unprepared.

In Plato's story, the central obstacle to effective freedom is human ignorance, both personal and communal. And the most serious form of this obstacle is ignorance of our own ignorance.[22] This is the formidable obstacle confronting those who seek to turn the prisoners around. They simply do not want to see, or believe, that they need to be turned. When Plato's myth of the cave is opposed to Rousseau's myth of the state of nature, we find the following critical contrasts. According to Plato, no one can be effectively free who is not wise, who does not know and love what is truly good. But no one can be good, who is not virtuous, who has not been liberated from ignorance and learned to distinguish real from apparent things and values. But no one can be virtuous who has not been effectively educated, that is educated for the two complementary stages of human freedom, in the double sense of being liberated from ignorance and empowered with authentic knowledge. In addition, it is the responsibility of those who have gradually and painfully become free to transform their original community, by engaging in the effort to liberate their peers, even at the cost of their own lives. To be genuinely good, it is not enough personally to seek wisdom; you must then freely share with others the discoveries you find.

Those familiar with the life story of Socrates know that Plato's myth of the cave is also a dramatic image of Socrates' memorable life and death.[23] Socrates was an Athenian citizen who slowly discovered his own ignorance and tried to help his fellow citizens discover theirs. They were not grateful for his efforts and eventually condemned him to death, on the capital charges of impiety and corruption of the young. At his trial, Socrates compared himself to a gadfly who kept buzzing around the lazy horse that was Athens, keeping it from spiritually falling asleep, until it deliberately silenced him with hemlock.[24]

The important ambiguity in Plato's story emerges when we identify Socrates with the liberated prisoner in the story. According to the myth, the prisoner who is compelled to return to the cave had seen, and therefore known, the Good, and then returned to the *polis* with this ultimate knowledge. In Platonic terms, such a person would be wise, knowing the Good and knowing its governing influence throughout all levels of existence. But was Socrates himself actually wise? Did he really experience the vision of the Good; and was the impressive freedom Socrates regularly displayed in the dialogues a freedom based on comprehensive wisdom? Or was Socrates, as he called himself, a philosopher, a lover of wisdom, one who sought the Good, knowing that he did not yet know it? He once admitted that he was the wisest man in Athens, but only because he actually knew that he was not wise, whereas those like Protagoras, who were publicly reputed to be wise, did not.[25]

These are not scholarly questions to be settled by experts in Platonic thought, but questions of central importance to the themes of this book. Can liberal education really hope to make us wise, to bring us to a definitive and certain knowledge of the Good? Is comprehensive wisdom one of the virtues necessary for effective freedom and authentic community? Should we expect a liberal education to make us permanently wise, or, rather, to make us philosophers, in the specific Socratic sense, ardent lovers of wisdom who actively seek wisdom with our whole being, but who never bring our lifelong search to a temporal close?

I don't have decisive answers to these important questions, but I do have several thoughts about them that I shall freely share with you. My view of the human being is a composite of Epimetheus and Prometheus, a being who regularly lives between hindsight and foresight. Combining them together presents an image of human life, which mixes light and darkness, wisdom and ignorance, precisely the combination Socrates claimed was essential to philosophy. My Socrates, unlike the liberated prisoner in the cave story, has made the critical discovery that no human being is wise, that final wisdom is a prerogative of the divine. This humbling discovery is not discouraging, however, for it is in truth an essential insight into the human condition we commonly share. But it is crucial how each person responds concretely to this liberating insight. If human beings are not wise, if they do not know by an enduring or recurring intuition what is good, then how should they actually live? Should we limit ourselves to the arts of survival and the interpersonal control of others, as we are urged to do by Protagoras and his many sophistic descendants; should we seek liberation from the incompleteness of intellectual knowledge by giving primacy to our spontaneous sensual impulses as urged by Rousseau; or should we, as ardent lovers do, use every resource at our command to pursue our genuine beloved, wisdom?

Should we, in a word, be educated for the philosophical life, the life of continuous inquiry, what Socrates called "the examined life," the genuinely human life?[26] Different answers to these inescapable questions determine different approaches to liberal education and effective freedom. Let me share with you now, my answer and my personal approach to liberal learning and teaching. I see liberal education as primarily a form of ethical education, not in the sense that it tells you all that is good, but rather that it seeks to develop within you the powers we need to conduct authentic and effective dialogues, both within ourselves and with our fellow humans. For beings like us, who are not wise but who long for wisdom, the norms of authentic dialogue are the norms of the good life. Dialogue is a form of mutual communication between the different parts of the self or between different selves, in which genuine persuasion, rather than proof, command, coercion, or deception, is the operative norm. In the dialogues with ourselves, through which we reach the defining decisions of our lives, it is essential that all our voices be heard, and that they be articulate. Sensibility, intelligence, good will, faith, the voices of the heart, all must be heard and responded to sympathetically, if these critical decisions are to enlist the loyalty of the whole person. The temptation here is always one of tyranny, of trying to have by one means what can only be had in some other way.[27] It is naïve to think that the different parts of the self are naturally articulate. Stammering, in fact, is our native form of eloquence. So, we need to be educated before we can understand the symbolism of images and feelings, the conceptual distinctions introduced by intelligence, the demand for sufficient evidence required by critical judgment, and the courage, fairness, and humility demanded by responsible action.

The purpose of liberal education is to cultivate our powers of genuine discernment; not the power to rule, manipulate, deceive or coerce, but the power to persuade and be persuaded by others, fairly, openly, humbly, and honestly. The powers required by open reciprocal dialogue, the kind of genuine discussion, which culminates in shared and responsible decisions, are those developed by a liberal education when it works. To what powers am I referring? Personal taste, practical insight, emotional and intellectual honesty, as well as the essential powers of receptivity and articulation: listening and reading with discrimination, sensitivity to bias in all its forms, a critical awareness of the past, a sense of continuity and change based on the personal and critical appropriation of one's traditions. I don't mean to offer you a complete catalogue of virtues, but liberal education is committed to human wholeness, and these virtues are essential parts of that slowly emerging whole. What the liberal spirit abhors is tyranny or impotence in dialogue, both of which are traceable to the lack of these developed powers, to the failure of our education, to the curtailment of authentic human freedom.

Given the complex conditions on which it depends, human dialogue is always a risk, an adventure, not a route to certainty. It is a path into the darkness to which we bring all the light that we can. Two miraculous human capacities sustain it through good times and bad: our power to make and keep promises, and our ability to forgive and be forgiven.[28] We should promise to be faithful to the different communities of dialogue to which we belong, especially when they arrive at mistaken decisions, and we are tempted to desert them for celebrated authorities (experts or gurus) or coercive institutions which claim to be more secure. Because dialogue is a human way of reaching decisions about what is good, a way that combines light and darkness, it can easily lead to errors of judgment. But this is where our power to forgive becomes critical. All of us are sometimes Epimetheus and sometimes Prometheus. When we are victims of another's errors and failures, will we have the human wisdom and depth to reenter community with those who have trespassed against us? And when it is our turn to be Epimetheus, a turn which occurs far too often, will we have the humility to accept the forgiveness of those we have harmed? Our capacity for promising gives us reason to believe that we belong to an ongoing community of learners and discoverers, students and teachers, including the dead and unborn, all of whom could/should be seeking wisdom together. And our capacity for forgiveness prevents that community from becoming a place of grievance and revenge when the conflicting purposes of fallible and flawed human beings intersect.[29]

At the beginning of this chapter, I promised to tell a concluding story, and now I shall honor my promise. This is a story I learned from a former teacher,

John Dunne, with whom I studied at the University of Notre Dame. Dunne's story represents an important variation on Plato's cave myth, a variation I've slowly learned to accept. The story, yet another creation myth, is called the parable of the mountain.[30]

We human beings are born into a valley, which exists at the base of a tall mountain. When we are young, we enjoy living in the valley, but as we grow into adolescence and adulthood, we discover that the valley contains loss, suffering, disappointment and death, as well as love and joy. This discovery is often hard to accept, and many of us begin to wonder whether life might be better, happier, outside the valley, living at the crest of the mountain. We hear stories that God lives at the top of the mountain, and that where God lives there is no suffering, no famine, war, pestilence, or death. And some of our teachers and sages insist that God exists beyond suffering because God is omniscient and omnipotent. Possessed of unlimited knowledge and power, God is able to control life on the mountaintop so that suffering and death cannot enter there.

At a certain point, some young people, never too many, begin to leave the valley and climb the mountain. It is unclear, as they leave, whether they are retreating from suffering or actively searching for knowledge.[31] Most give up and turn back from the steep climb, but one person, the hero of our story, makes it all the way to the summit. That is, she gains the kind of knowledge and the kind of power that could protect a human being from suffering and death. But at the same time, she makes a surprising discovery, the summit of the mountain is empty. God is not there. The stories she had heard about God living alone and secure on the mountain top are apparently not true. And yet, she does find some footsteps, God's footsteps perhaps, which pass back down the mountain in the direction from which she came. As she was seeking God, or at least a familiar image of God, by leaving the valley, perhaps God was seeking us by freely entering it. As she was fleeing the valley to avoid suffering and loss, perhaps God was freely accepting suffering and death, without using divine power to overcome or destroy them. Perhaps, in freely leaving the mountaintop God had voluntarily surrendered divine power, taking the humble form of a human being, like us in all things except sin.[32]

At the crest of the mountain, our hero does not have a vision of the Good, as in Plato's story, but a series of questions, of provocative maybes, that lead her to rethink the stories we hear and tell about God. Reflecting on these stories and her own distinctive experience, she decides to re-enter the valley, seeing it now from a new and different perspective, perhaps ready to find God and the good within sadness and joy, rather than above and beyond them. As we conclude this searching reflection on education, knowledge, community, and freedom, let us leave our hero pondering all of these questions. Let us leave her in the spirit of wonder, the spirit in which philosophy originally began and continues to begin. And as long as philosophy remains truly alive, the sustaining spirit it shall never forsake.[33]

NOTES

1. *The Collected Dialogues of Plato* (Princeton: Princeton University Press, 1989) *Protagoras*, 308–52.

2. For Protagoras' creation story, see *Protagoras* 320d-329e.

3. For the myth of Prometheus, his gift and punishment, see Jean Pierre Vernant, *The Myth of Prometheus, Myth and Society in Ancient Greece.*

4. For Zeus' gift of the political arts, see *Protagoras* 322c-323e.

5. For Protagoras' distinction between the specialized and political arts, see *Protagoras* 323–27.

6. See Michael Sandel's recent criticism of the meritocratic ideal, Sandel, *The Tyranny of Merit: What's Become of the Common Good?* (New York: Macmillan, 2020).

7. For Socrates' criticism of Protagoras' argument, see *Protagoras* 329–35.

8. See Rousseau, *The Social Contract.*

9. In the following paragraphs, I am summarizing Rousseau's argument in *The Second Discourse on Inequality.*

10. In Part I of *The Second Discourse*, Rousseau describes the life of the "natural man" in the state of nature. In Part II, he offers a genetic account of the increasing development of inequality within human society.

11. Surprisingly, almost nothing is said about the care and nurture of infant children until they reach the stage of natural self-sufficiency.

12. Much of Part I is devoted to showing how these "moral attributes" can be found in humans apart from the education they receive in civil society.

13. In Rousseau's account of freedom as "negative liberty," it is freedom from authority as such, not freedom from illegitimate and despotic authority, that matters.

14. In marked contrast to Aristotle and the classical tradition, "nature" and "reason" are oppositional terms. Reason, as conceived by Rousseau, is not part of our original human nature.

15. In fact, for Rousseau, it is the social institutions founded "to cultivate the arts and virtues" that are the principal sources of human inequality.

16. *Republic* VII, 514a.

17. *Republic* VII, 515a.

18. *Republic* VII, 515c.

19. *Republic* VII, 516b.

20. *Republic* VII 517a.

21. *Republic* VII 517a–520b.

22. This serves to explain the twofold liberation achieved by liberal education: first, liberation from the ignorance of our own ignorance that is sustained by a non-virtuous society, and then liberation from the greater ignorance of intelligible being and the good.

23. For the trial, conviction and death of Socrates, see Plato's *Apology, Crito, and Phaedo*.

24. *Apology* 30e-31a.

25. This claim is at the heart of Socrates' self-defense in the *Apology*.

26. The whole of Plato's *Apology* can be read as a defense of "the examined life."

27. The insight derives from Pascal.

28. See Hannah Arendt, *The Human Condition*, 236–47.

29. The appropriate emphasis on human finitude and fallibility does not preclude our personal and communal capacity for self-transcendence, but it does reveal why the arts and virtues are so important in enabling that high and essential achievement.

30. The Parable of the Mountain can be found in John Dunne's *The Way of all the Earth*, 14–23.

31. In the parable, Dunne emphasizes that our reasons for leaving the valley are mixed, an energizing combination of yearning and fear.

32. See St. Paul, *Epistle to the Hebrews* 4:15.

33. Aristotle, *Metaphysics,* Book I.

Chapter 9

Our Common Struggle
with Unwelcome Truths

We are living simultaneously through several critical challenges, political, cultural, religious, and intellectual.

A critical period in the history of American democracy in which deliberate voter suppression, partisan gerrymandering, the corrupting influence of "dark money," and pervasive lying and disinformation make just and responsible democratic governance nearly impossible.

In the field of international relations, where democratic and despotic regimes on every continent are regularly in conflict with each other. And even within nominal democracies, autocratic nationalists, anti-government populists, and their unprincipled political allies threaten the rights and liberties of their fellow citizens.

In the history of civic education, where the liberal arts and virtues, and the norms, principles, and aspirations essential to collaborative democratic inquiry and dialogue are openly rejected or repeatedly ignored.

In the history of culture and cooperative inquiry, where the public role of religion in a free society is deeply contested, where the historic partnership of science and technology produces very uneven results, and where hostility to specialized knowledge and its essential role in shaping sound public policies is deliberately encouraged for narrow partisan ends.

Finally, responsible and effective self-government, in political, religious and educational communities, cannot succeed without a common set of facts, a shared agreement about essential public goods, and a deliberative process that seeks persuasion and consensus through genuinely civil dialogue and argument. However, each of these essential requirements of an authentic deliberative community is now clearly in danger.

What then can the responsible citizen do, who clearly perceives these dangers, and seeks to address them effectively in his/her own speech and conduct? Based on long years of personal experience and considerable historical reflection, let me propose the following democratic imperatives.

Four essential imperatives to foster collaborative and fruitful dialogues across differences in belief, background, and cultural and political outlook.

1. Seek the fullness of truth in a spirit of humility and realism, clearly acknowledging the singular importance of factual and evaluative truth, and the finitude and fallibility of all human inquiry. And with the consistent purpose of enlarging our communal understanding, not winning a cultural or political contest. Human learning and teaching, in all domains of inquiry, should be cooperative, not competitive, in spirit; sourced in our common desire to understand reality, not our emotional need for certainty and power.[1]
2. Speak the truth, as you now understand it, in a spirit of genuine friendship. Whitehead wisely distinguished between the opinions we hold, and the way in which we hold them.[2] The same distinction applies to the manner, the spirit, in which we share what we have learned or believe with others, particularly those who initially distrust or oppose us.
3. Let us share the common world that truth reveals in a spirit of cooperative solidarity. For solidarity, genuine civic friendship, is, perhaps, the most inclusive, and least jealous, form of love we humans enjoy.[3]

All three imperatives clearly acknowledge the powerful influence of emotions on our thought, speech, action, and interaction with others. This is particularly true of fear, anger, and resentment. Fear that what we and others prize and value is seriously threatened; anger, based on the belief that the threats come from those who are hostile to our legitimate concerns; and resentment, based on the assumption that our political and cultural rivals scorn us as ignorant, uneducated, old-fashioned, and ill informed. When these emotions dominate our public discourse, reaching a shared understanding together becomes exceedingly difficult, if not impossible.

Human life is marked by constant change, though the pace of change is historically variable. Sometimes, change brings evident development and growth; sometimes, the real or apparent loss of what we greatly value. For example, threats to those we love; our sources of "self-respect"; to the way of life that has allowed us to feel at home and of worth in the world. Today, demagogues, self-interested conmen, "spin doctors," tyrants, and their media allies deliberately exploit these fears by blaming the perceived loss or injury on "others": foreigners, refugees, the federal government; educated or cultural "elites"; those who allegedly scorn us and our traditional way of life.

4. So, the fourth imperative is especially critical now: Be particularly attentive and resistant to the despot's calculated and cynical reliance on available "scapegoats."[4]

Most personal and historical change brings with it both gain and loss. This is particularly true of the changes in Western societies since the 1960s. Cultural changes in the family and sexual morality; political changes in the composition, aims, and priorities of our major political parties; the dramatic economic changes caused by "globalization," advanced technology, and international trade; generational changes separating the sensibilities of the old and young; international changes in the balance of power since the end of the "Cold War"; the complex and evolving secularization of Western culture; the very mixed blessings of pervasive social media. Responding wisely and effectively to these interdependent fields of change requires all the virtues I outlined in our four imperatives: humility, generosity, practical wisdom, critical realism, and civic friendship.

But sadly, we are not born with any of these virtues. They have to be actively cultivated by the practice of EDUCATION in the fullest sense: at home; at school; in college; in our places of worship; on athletic teams; with our many friends; at our places of work; in what we read, see, and hear on a regular basis: through attentive experience of the creative arts and the many sources of credible information, analysis, and narrative on which we regularly rely. For without these critical virtues, we are likely to respond to unwelcome truths with denial, diversion, the deliberate "discrediting" of those who tell us what we do not want to hear, accept, or live by.

In our time of deliberately cultivated mistrust by dangerous demagogues, like Trump and his cynical political allies, and the numerous conmen who manipulate the content of social media, we are actively led into a world of continuous lies, blame, conspiracies, and open hostility and contempt. This is particularly true of the right-wing propaganda webs seeking to discredit the efficacy of vaccines, the gravity of climate change, the integrity of our elections; the scandals of economic inequality and racial injustice, and critical accounts of our checkered national and spiritual histories.

But it is also true of some parts of the "progressive left" who forget that politics is based on the art of persuasion, that effective and enduring political coalitions develop by addition, not subtraction; and that a democratic politics of "liberty and justice for all" requires "the long slow boring of hard boards" (Max Weber).[5] In my long years as a voting citizen, 1964 until now, the "progressive left" has often been its own worst enemy in achieving the more just society it rightly seeks.

Engaged pluralism: "Feelings and opinions are recruited, the heart is enlarged, and the mind developed, only by the reciprocal influence of human beings on one another." Alexis de Tocqueville, *Democracy in America*.[6]

Genuine national, cultural, and spiritual unity does not require uniformity of opinion and judgment. But it does require the fruitful and civil interaction and dialogue of the diverse groups within American society. Women and men; young and old; religious and skeptical; traditional and innovative; affluent and poor; and the full range of racial and ethnic communities that stretch from the Atlantic to the Pacific. "E pluribus unum" is the declaration of a sustained and responsible democratic process, not of a fixed and static result. The reciprocal and collaborative engagement of all citizens in our pluralistic democracy is the only way to restore genuine and sustainable American unity. But that engagement is impossible unless we foster, prize, and reliably exercise the essential virtues of a liberal and democratic education.

A committed teacher, parent, and citizen, I have written this book as a personal contribution to that essential, unfinished and gravely challenged American dialogue.

Thank you for your attention.

NOTES

1. The desire to understand experience exists in all human beings. It develops through learning, a self-correcting process that draws on one's own revisable insights and the revisable insights of so many others. See Bernard Lonergan's *Insight: A Study in Human Understanding*.

2. Alfred North Whitehead develops this important distinction in *Science and the Modern World* and *Adventures of Ideas*.

3. C. S. Lewis describes friendship as "the least jealous form of love" in his book, *The Four Loves*, Harper Collins, 1960.

4. See Rene Girard's important study of *Scapegoats,* Johns Hopkins Press, 1981.

5. See Max Weber, *The Vocation Lectures*, including *Politics as a Vocation*, Hackett Classics. See also E. J. Dionne's recent work, *Code Red*, where he argues for the needed political collaboration of moderates and progressives in this era of Trump's threatening demagoguery.

6. Alexis de Tocqueville, *Democracy in America*, Book II, chapter 5.

Bibliography

Abbey, Ruth. *Charles Taylor*. Princeton: Princeton University Press, 2000.

Allen, Anita and Regan, Milton editors. *Debating Democracy's Discontent*. New York: Oxford University Press, 1998.

Aquinas. *Basic Writings of Thomas Aquinas*, Volumes 1 and 2. Editor, Anton Pegis. New York: Random House, 1945.

Arendt, Hannah. *Between Past and Future*. New York: Viking Press, 1968.

Arendt, Hannah. *Crises of the Republic*. New York: Harcourt Brace Jovanovich, 1972.

Arendt, Hannah. *The Human Condition*. Chicago: University of Chicago Press, 1958.

Arendt, Hannah. *Lectures on Kant's Political Philosophy*. Chicago: University of Chicago Press, 1982.

Arendt, Hannah. *On Revolution*. New York: Viking Press, 1963.

Arendt, Hannah. *The Origins of Totalitarianism*. New York: Meridian Books, 1958.

Aristotle. *The Basic Works of Aristotle*. Edited by Richard McKeon. New York: Random House, 1941.

Augustine. *The City of God*. New York: Modern Library, 1950.

Augustine. *Confessions*. New York: Penguin, 1961.

Bacon, Francis. *Novum Organon*. New York: Oxford University Press, 2004.

Barber, Benjamin. *Strong Democracy: Participatory Politics in a New Age*. Berkeley: University of California Press, 1984.

Bellah, Robert et al. *Habits of the Heart: Individualism and Commitment in American Life*. Berkeley: University of California Press, 1985.

Bellow, Saul. *Herzog*. New York: Penguin, 1996.

Bellow, Saul. *Mister Sammler's Planet*. New York: Penguin, 1995.

Berlin, Isaiah. *Four Essays on Liberty*. New York: Oxford University Press, 1969.

Butterfield, Herbert. *The Origins of Modern Science 1300-1800*. New York: Free Press, 1957.

Constant, Benjamin. *Political Writings*. Cambridge: Cambridge University Press, 1988.

Dahl, Robert. *On Democracy*. New Haven: Yale University Press, 1989.

Darwin, Charles. *The Origin of Species*. New York: Dutton, 1928.

Delbanco, Andrew. *College*. Princeton: Princeton University Press, 2014.

Descartes, Rene. *The Philosophical Works of Descartes*. Volumes 1 and 2. New York: Cambridge University Press, 1972.

Dewey, John. *The Influence of Darwin on Philosophy*. New York: Peter Smith, 1951.

Dilthey, Wilhelm. *Introduction to the Human Sciences*. Princeton: Princeton University Press, 1989.

Dionne Jr, E. J. *Code Red*. New York: St Martin's Press, 2020.

Dionne Jr, E. J. *Why the Right Went Wrong*. New York: Simon and Schuster, 2016.

Dunne, John. *The City of the Gods*. New York: Macmillan, 1965.

Dunne, John. *Reasons of the Heart*. Notre Dame: University of Notre Dame Press, 1979.

Dunne, John. *A Search for God in Time and Memory*. New York: Macmillan, 1969.

Dunne, John. *The Way of All the Earth*. Notre Dame: University of Notre Dame Press, 1978.

Ellis, Joseph. *American Dialogue*. New York: Vintage Books, 2018.

Erikson, Erik. *Identity, Youth and Crisis*. New York: Norton, 1968.

Etzioni, Amitai. *New Communitarian Thinking*. Charlottesville: University of Virginia Press, 1995.

The Federalist Papers (James Madison, Alexander Hamilton, John Jay). New York: Penguin Classics, 1987.

Freud, Sigmund. Vol. 54 of *Great Books of the Western World*. Chicago: Encyclopedia Britannica, 1952.

Gadamer, Hans. *Truth and Method*. London: Sheed and Ward, 1975.

Galilei, Galileo. *Dialogue Concerning the Two Chief World Systems, Ptolemaic and Copernican*. Berkeley: University of California Press, 1953.

Galston, William. *Anti-Pluralism*. New Haven: Yale University Press, 2018.

Girard, Rene. *The Scapegoat*. Baltimore: Johns Hopkins University Press, 1986.

Havel, Vaclav. *Summer Meditations*. New York: Vintage Books, 1992.

Hegel, G.W.F. *Reason in History*. Indianapolis: Library of the Liberal Arts, 1953.

Heilbroner, Robert. *The Worldly Philosophers*. New York: Simon and Schuster, 1986.

Hirschman, Albert. *The Passions and the Interests*. Princeton: Princeton University Press, 1977.

Hollenbach, David. *The Common Good and Christian Ethics*. Cambridge: Cambridge University Press, 2002.

Honohan, Iseult. *Civic Republicanism*. London: Routledge, 2002.

Hume, David. *An Inquiry Concerning Human Understanding*. Indianapolis: Library of Liberal Arts, 1955.

Jaeger, Werner. *Paideia*, Vols 1-3. New York: Oxford University Press, 1939.

Kant, Immanuel. *Critique of Practical Reason*. New York: Bobbs Merrill, 1956.

Kant, Immanuel. *Critique of Pure Reason*. New York: St Martin's Press, 1961.

Kierkegaard, Soren. *Philosophical Fragments*. Princeton: Princeton University Press, 1941.

Kolakowski, Lezek. *Modernity on Endless Trial*. Chicago: University of Chicago Press, 1990.

Koyre, Alexandre. *From the Closed World to the Infinite Universe*. New York: Harper and Brothers, 1958.

Kronman, Anthony. *Education's End*. New Haven: Yale University Press, 2007.

Kuhn, Thomas. *The Structure of Scientific Revolutions*. Chicago: Chicago University Press, 1970.

Levitsky, Steven and Ziblatt, Daniel. *How Democracies Die*. New York: Crown Publishing, 2018.

Lincoln, Abraham. *Lincoln on Democracy*. New York: Harper Collins, 1990.

Lobkowicz, Nicholas. *Theory and Practice. History of a Concept from Aristotle to Marx*. Notre Dame: University of Notre Dame Press, 1967.

Locke, John. *An Essay Concerning Human Understanding*. Indianapolis: Hackett Publishing, 1996.

Lonergan, Bernard. *Collection, Collected Works of Lonergan, Vol 4*. Toronto: University of Toronto Press, 1988.

Lonergan, Bernard. *Insight: A Study in Human Understanding*. New York: Harper and Row, 1978.

Lonergan, Bernard. *Method in Theology*. New York: Herder and Herder, 1972.

Lonergan, Bernard. *A Second Collection*. Philadelphia: The Westminster Press, 1974.

Lonergan, Bernard. *A Third Collection*. New York: Paulist Press, 1985.

MacIntyre, Alasdair. *After Virtue*. Notre Dame: University of Notre Dame Press, 1981.

MacIntyre, Alasdair. *Three Rival Versions of Moral Inquiry*. Notre Dame: University of Notre Dame Press, 1990.

Macpherson, C. B. *The Political Theory of Possessive Individualism*. New York: Oxford University Press, 1962.

Mann, Thomas and Ornstein, Norman. *It's Even Worse Than It Looks*. New York: Basic Books, 2012.

Mann, Thomas and Ornstein, Norman. *It's Even Worse Than It Was*. New York: Basic Books, 2016.

Marx, Karl. *Karl Marx: Selected Writings*. New York: Oxford University Press, 1977.

McCarthy, Michael. *Authenticity as Self-Transcendence*. Notre Dame: University of Notre Dame Press, 2016.

McCarthy, Michael. *The Crisis of Philosophy*. Albany: SUNY Press, 1990.

McCarthy, Michael. *Toward a Catholic Christianity*. Lanham, MD: Lexington Books, 2017.

McCarthy, Michael. *The Political Humanism of Hannah Arendt*. Lanham, MD: Lexington Books, 2012.

Milbank, Dana. *The Destructionists*. New York: Doubleday, 2022.

Mill, John Stuart. *On Liberty*. Indianapolis: Hackett, 1978.

Montesquieu, Charles. *The Spirit of Laws*. Cambridge: Cambridge University Press, 1989.

Murdoch, Iris. *Metaphysics as a Guide to Morals*. New York; Penguin, 1992.

Murdoch, Iris. *The Sovereignty of Good*. New York: Schocken Books, 1971.

Murray, John Courtney. *We Hold These Truths*. New York: Sheed and Ward, 1960.

Newman, John Henry. *The Idea of a University*. Notre Dame: University of Notre Dame Press, 2016.

Niebuhr, Reinhold. *Moral Man and Immoral Society*. New York: Charles Scribner's Sons, 1964.

Nietzsche, Friedrich. *The Genealogy of Morals: A Polemic*. New York: Russell and Russell, 1964.

Packer, George. *Our Last Best Hope*. New York: Farrar, Straus and Giroux, 2022.

Pascal, Blaise. *Pensées*. New York: Penguin Books, 1966.

Plato. *The Collected Dialogues*. Bollingen Series. Princeton: Princeton University Press, 1961.

Polanyi, Michael. *Personal Knowledge*. Chicago: University of Chicago Press, 1958.

Putnam, Robert. *Bowling Alone*. New York: Simon and Schuster, 2000.

Rawls, John. *A Theory of Justice*. Cambridge, MA: Harvard University Press, 1971.

Ricoeur, Paul. *Freud and Philosophy: An Essay on Interpretation*. New Haven: Yale University Press, 1970.

Ricoeur, Paul. *Ideology and Utopia*. New York: Columbia University Press, 1986.

Ricoeur, Paul. *Time and Narrative*. Chicago: University of Chicago Press, 1984.

Rorty, Richard. *The Linguistic Turn*. Chicago: University of Chicago Press, 1967.

Rorty, Richard. *Philosophy and the Mirror of Nature*. Princeton: Princeton University Press,1979.

Rousseau, Jean Jacques. *The First and Second Discourses*. New York: St Martin's Press, 1964.

Rousseau, Jean Jacques. *The Social Contract and other later Political Writings*. New York: Cambridge University, 1997.

Sandel, Michael. *Democracy's Discontent*. Cambridge: Harvard University Press, 1996.

Sandel, Michael. *Liberalism and the Theory of Justice*. Cambridge: Harvard University Press, 1995.

Sandel, Michael. *The Tyranny of Merit*. New York: Farrar, Straus and Giroux, 2020.

Smith, Adam. *The Wealth of Nations*. Oxford: Clarendon Press, 1976.

Taylor, Charles. *A Secular Age*. Cambridge: Harvard University Press, 2007.

Taylor, Charles. *The Ethics of Authenticity*. Cambridge: Harvard University Press, 1991.

Taylor, Charles. *Hegel in Modern Society*. New York: Cambridge University Press, 1979.

Taylor, Charles. *Philosophical Arguments*. Cambridge: Harvard University Press, 1995.

Taylor, Charles. *Philosophical Papers, Vols 1 and 2*. Cambridge: Cambridge University Press, 1992.

Taylor, Charles. *Sources of the Self*. Cambridge: Harvard University Press, 1989.

Tocqueville, Alexis de. *Democracy in America, Vols 1 and 2*. New York: Vintage Books, 1961.

Trilling, Lionel. *Sincerity and Authenticity*. Cambridge: Harvard University Press, 1972.

Tussman, Joseph. *An Experiment at Berkeley*. New York: Oxford University Press, 1969.

Voegelin, Eric. *The World of the Polis*. Baton Rouge: Louisiana State University Press, 1957.

Weber, Max. *The Essential Weber*. New York: Oxford University Press, 1958.

Whitehead, A. N. *Aims of Education*. New York: Mentor, 1967.

Whitehead, A. N. *Adventures of Ideas*. New York: Macmillan, 1933.

Whitehead, A. N. *Science and the Modern World*. New York: New American Library, 1954.

Wood, Gordon. *The Radicalism of the American Revolution*. New York: Vintage, 1993.

Index

About the Author

Michael H. McCarthy, Professor Emeritus of Philosophy, has been a teacher and scholar at Vassar College for fifty-five years. A graduate of Notre Dame and Yale, he has authored or co-authored seven books, including *The Crisis of Philosophy, The Political Humanism of Hannah Arendt, Authenticity as Self-Transcendence: The Enduring Insights of Bernard Lonergan*, and *Toward a Catholic Christianity: A Study in Critical Belonging*.

Professor McCarthy, a former fellow at the Woodstock Theological Center and a board member of the Lonergan Institute at Boston College, has lectured widely throughout the United States and abroad on cognitional, ethical, and political topics and themes. He has just completed work on a new book, entitled *Liberal Education and Democratic Citizenship*, about several grave crises now confronting American democracy. When the muse visits, he also writes poems for family and friends, seeking to turn the truth of our lives into poetry.

As learner, teacher, and citizen, he has loved being an active member of Vassar's thriving philosophical community.